W9-BLZ-331

Martha Stewart's
Dinner at Home

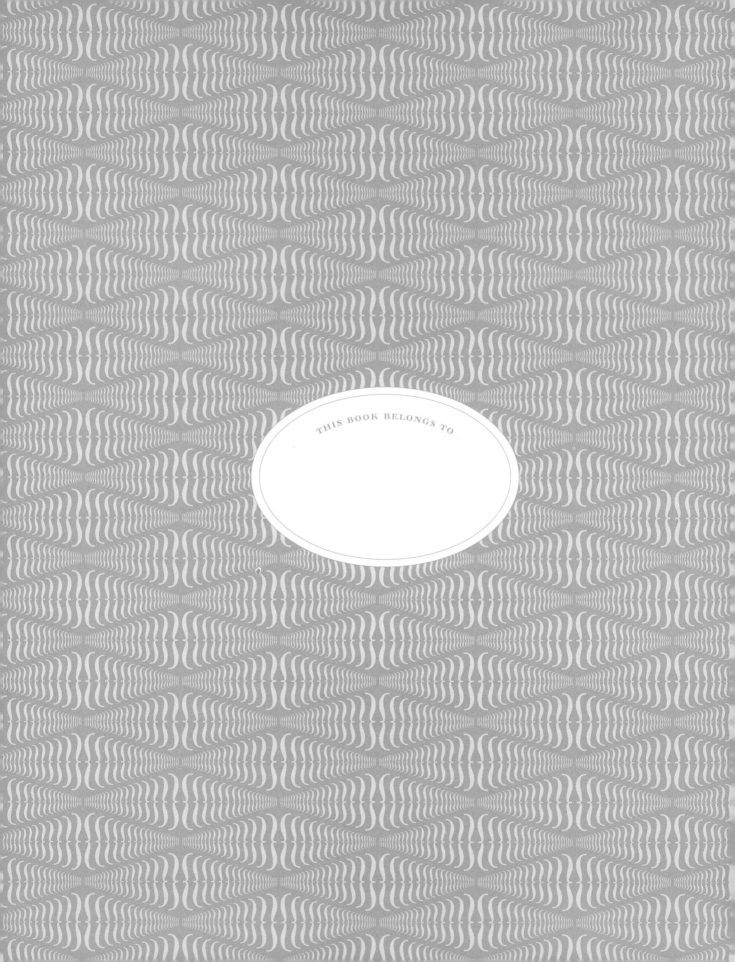

THIS BOOK BELONGS TO

Martha Stewart's Dinner at Home

52 QUICK MEALS TO COOK FOR FAMILY & FRIENDS

Clarkson Potter/Publishers
New York

Copyright © 2009 by Martha Stewart Living Omnimedia Inc.

All rights reserved.
Published in the United States by Clarkson Potter/Publishers,
an imprint of the Crown Publishing Group,
a division of Random House, Inc., New York.
www.crownpublishing.com
www.clarksonpotter.com

Clarkson N. Potter is a trademark and Potter with colophon is a
registered trademark of Random House, Inc.

Some photographs and recipes originally appeared in
Martha Stewart Living publications.

Library of Congress Cataloging-in-Publication Data
Stewart, Martha.
[Dinner at Home]
Martha Stewart's Dinner at Home:
52 Quick Meals to Cook for Family & Friends / Martha Stewart.—1st ed.
1. Dinners and dining. 2. Menus. I. Title. II. Title: Dinner at home.
TX737.S8565 2009
641.5—dc22   2008051519

ISBN 978-0-307-39645-7

Printed in China

Design by Matthew Papa

Photograph credits appear on page 266.

10 9 8 7 6 5 4 3 2 1

First Edition

To all homemakers in America,
pressed for time
yet caring for their families

introduction

I wrote my first *Quick Cook* book in 1983, and it was an instant "must have" for home cooks—popular because it struck a chord with people like me, busy homemakers who worked, raised families, maintained homes, and loved good, quickly prepared, interesting food. *Quick Cook Menus* and *Healthy Quick Cook* followed, two books that are still on my shelf and on cookbook shelves everywhere because they provide suggestions for menu planning and strategy, as well as excellent recipes that use a wide variety of easily available ingredients. The daily "what to have for dinner" conundrum was solved for many of us. Our monthly magazine, *Martha Stewart Living*, also adopted the formula of the "Quick Cook" menu—four easy recipes for a healthy, delicious meal that could be prepared in about an hour—in a column that has become another anticipated "must have" for our readers.

Now, with this book, I am thrilled to present a brand-new, exciting, and mouthwatering compilation of menus. Arranged seasonally to take advantage of what's in the market, these meals are accessible, but they also satisfy our desire for an even broader range of foodstuffs. Fava beans, dandelion greens, heirloom tomatoes, bok choy, Vidalia onions, coconut milk, and couscous, to name just a few, are wonderfully flavorful ingredients that have found their way into supermarkets and restaurants everywhere. As the world becomes an even "flatter" table, we are being introduced to the flavors and foods of an increasingly expansive landscape, and these inventive and delightful menus and recipes take full advantage of that wonderful availability.

I urge you to use this book strategically. Study the lists of menus following each season's opener (pages 12–13, 74–75, 138–139, and 200–201), then choose meals or individual recipes that fit your needs and make the best use of your pantry, refrigerator, and freezer. I think you will find that you and your family will benefit greatly from this new collection of recipes, which are sure to become favorites in your own personal repertoire.

Martha Stewart

spring

With one foot still planted in winter, early spring straddles the seasons. Depending on where you live, you might still need to rely on storage produce, such as potatoes and apples, to supplement local vegetables and fruits just now cropping up in the produce aisle. Whatever your particular region, the following menus will help you make the transition from heartier stews and braises to fresher, brighter dishes to reflect the spirit of renewal that comes with this time of year. The first dinner features asparagus, peas, mint, and rhubarb—a few of the more eagerly anticipated arrivals. With seared baby lamb chops as the main course, it's special enough to serve at an Easter or a Mother's Day celebration, or any other festive occasion. Pasta, a year-round staple, is paired with fresh herbs in one menu, and mint pesto and fava beans in another, for of-the-moment flavors. Elsewhere you'll find ways to make the most of late-season finery in utterly accessible menus with Mediterranean, Asian, and Latin American flavors, plus other dishes that may feel closer to home. And when strawberries make their first appearance, you'll want to use them to embellish a bread and butter pudding for a fitting finale to supper.

spring menus

This meal captures the essence of spring on a plate—in this case, a French terra-cotta plate inspired by 18th-century designs. Lamb is a traditional main course at this time of year; here it is joined by asparagus and other seasonal ingredients, whose fresh flavors stand out in dishes that involve little cooking and minimal seasoning.

Baby Lamb Chops with Lemon Strips
Asparagus with Aïoli
Quinoa, Pea, and Mint Salad
Vanilla-Poached Rhubarb

PREPARATION SCHEDULE

1. Poach rhubarb; whip fromage blanc, and chill in the refrigerator.

2. Make aïoli; cover and refrigerate.

3. Prepare the quinoa salad (do not add mint); blanch asparagus.

4. Cook lamb. Mix mint into quinoa salad.

5. Assemble dessert just before serving.

Baby Lamb Chops with Lemon Strips

Baby lamb chops are very quick to cook and dainty to eat; three of them make a nice serving size for dinner. Larger chops, such as loin, can be substituted; plan on two per person, and cook four to six minutes per side for medium-rare. Serves 4

- 3 tablespoons olive oil
- 12 baby lamb chops (each about 3 ounces and 1 inch thick)
  Coarse salt and freshly ground pepper
- 1 lemon

Use a citrus zester to remove peel from lemon (leaving bitter white pith behind) in very fine strips. Then halve lemon and squeeze out juice.

Heat the oil in a large sauté pan over high. Pat dry lamb with paper towels, and season both sides with salt and pepper. When oil is hot but not smoking, add the lamb, working in batches to avoid crowding. Reduce heat to medium-high; cook until browned, about 2 minutes per side, turning chops once with tongs and transferring all but last batch to a platter.

Once the last batch has been browned, return all lamb to the hot pan and add the lemon zest and juice. Toss quickly to coat lamb, and serve.

Asparagus with Aïoli

Aïoli, a garlic-flavored mayonnaise with origins in Provence, is traditionally enjoyed as a sauce for steamed vegetables and seafood; here it makes a luscious dip for asparagus. Serves 4

- Coarse salt and freshly ground pepper
- 1 bunch asparagus (about 1 pound), tough ends trimmed
- 1 large egg
- 1 garlic clove
- ½ cup safflower or other neutral-tasting oil
- ⅓ cup extra-virgin olive oil

Bring a large pot of water to a boil; add 2 tablespoons salt. Blanch the asparagus until bright green and crisp-tender, 2 to 4 minutes (depending on thickness of stalk). Remove with tongs and drain on a paper towel–lined baking sheet.

To make the aïoli, combine the egg and garlic with ½ teaspoon salt and ¼ teaspoon pepper in a food processor or mini-chopper; slowly add the safflower oil and then the olive oil in a steady stream, processing just until mixture is emulsified. Serve with asparagus. (Aïoli can be refrigerated up to 2 days in an airtight container.)

The eggs in this recipe are not fully cooked, so it should not be prepared for pregnant women, babies, young children, the elderly, or anyone whose health is compromised.

{ Crisp-tender spears of asparagus, along with a garlicky mayonnaise for dipping, doubles as a delicious appetizer. The small bowl is mid-19th-century transferware (peacock pattern).

Quinoa, Pea, and Mint Salad

Other grains, such as bulgur wheat or pearl barley, can be used in place of quinoa for this salad; follow the package instructions for cooking the grains for the appropriate length of time. You can vary the other ingredients, too, using fresh parsley instead of mint, and chopped scallions or cucumbers in place of peas (fold them in off the heat with the herbs). Serves 4

- 2   cups chicken stock, homemade (see page 260) or low-sodium store-bought
- 1   cup white quinoa, rinsed
- 1   cup shelled fresh green peas (from 1 pound in pods) or frozen peas (unthawed)
      Coarse salt and freshly ground pepper
- 3   tablespoons extra-virgin olive oil
- 3   tablespoons fresh mint leaves, torn if large

Bring stock and quinoa to a boil in a 2-quart saucepan. Reduce heat to a simmer; cover and cook 10 minutes, then add peas. Cook until quinoa is tender but still chewy and has absorbed the liquid, about 5 minutes more. Remove from heat, and let stand, covered, 5 minutes.

Season with salt and pepper, then stir in the oil. Transfer to a serving bowl and let cool slightly (about 5 minutes) before gently stirring in the mint. Serve salad warm or at room temperature.

About Quinoa

Quinoa (pronounced "KEEN-wah"), a nutty-flavored grain, is an excellent source of protein and is the only non-animal protein that contains all of the essential amino acids. Quinoa is also rich in calcium, iron, vitamin E, and B vitamins. Although often categorized with other cereal grains, such as corn and rice, quinoa is the seed of a leafy green vegetable—the *Chenopodium quinoa* plant —which means it's a great option for those with gluten sensitivities. The tiny seeds, which cook more quickly than long-grain rice, are available in various colors, but are most commonly found in white or red varieties at supermarkets and health-food stores.

About Rhubarb

Although it is a vegetable, rhubarb is more often cooked like a fruit, appearing in a range of desserts, including pies, cobblers, crisps, and compotes. The long, thick stalks are similar in shape to celery, and range in color from deep red to pale pink tinged with green. Rhubarb is at its peak in spring, when it can be readily found at grocery stores and farmers' markets. Choose crisp stalks that are about an inch wide, with no brown spots. Refrigerate rhubarb in a plastic bag for up to one week. When you're ready to use, rinse the rhubarb well, then trim and discard the bottoms, tops, and any leaves (which are toxic). If the stalks are stringy, peel them with a paring knife, as you would for celery.

Vanilla-Poached Rhubarb

Fromage blanc, a fresh cheese made from cow's milk, has a mild, tangy taste and a creamy texture. It can be found at specialty food stores and cheese shops. If you cannot find it, simply double the amount of heavy cream and proceed, beating with the sugar and vanilla until soft peaks form, then chill. Serves 4

For rhubarb
- 1 cup dry white wine
- ⅓ cup water
- ⅓ cup sugar
- ½ vanilla bean, split lengthwise and seeds scraped
- ½ pound rhubarb, trimmed and cut into 1-inch pieces (about 2 cups)

For cream
- ½ cup heavy cream
- 2 tablespoons sugar
- ½ vanilla bean, split lengthwise and seeds scraped
- 4 ounces fromage blanc (½ cup)

Poach rhubarb: Bring the wine, water, sugar, and vanilla-bean seeds to a boil in a medium saucepan over medium-high heat. Continue boiling 6 minutes, then add the rhubarb and reduce heat to a simmer; cook until rhubarb is just turning tender, about 2 minutes, tilting pan occasionally to coat the pieces with the poaching liquid. Remove from heat, and let cool completely.

Whip cream: With an electric mixer on medium-high speed, whisk the cream, sugar, and vanilla-bean seeds until medium-stiff peaks form. Add fromage blanc, and beat 1 minute more, or until mixture is still fluffy but will hold its shape. Transfer to a bowl and cover with plastic wrap; refrigerate 30 minutes, just until chilled.

To serve, spoon the cream mixture into small serving dishes. Using a slotted spoon, top each with some rhubarb, then drizzle with syrup.

{ Antique French jam jars are just right for serving old-fashioned spoon desserts that are sweet, tart, tangy, and creamy all at once. The subtle and distinctive flavor of vanilla bean permeates the dish, as the scraped seeds are used in both the poaching liquid for the rhubarb, which is drizzled on top, as well as the whipped cream underneath.

Spring Salad with Fresh Mozzarella
Turkey and Pancetta Meatballs
Pasta with Mint Pesto and Fava
Coffee Ice Cream Affogato

PREPARATION SCHEDULE

1. Blanch and peel fava beans; make pesto, and cover with oil.

2. Form and cook meatballs.

3. Boil pasta; assemble salad.

4. Toss pasta with pesto and fava beans; dress salad.

5. Prepare dessert just before serving.

Pasta with Mint Pesto and Fava

Here the pasta is topped with turkey and pancetta meatballs, but it also makes a delicious starter or light main course on its own. Fresh fava beans are found at specialty produce stores and farmers' markets for several weeks in the spring. If you can't find fresh favas, look for frozen (shelled) ones at many supermarkets and natural food stores; defrost according to package instructions. Serves 4

Coarse salt and freshly ground pepper
1 cup shelled fresh fava beans (about ½ pound in pod)
½ cup roasted unsalted almonds (about 2 ounces)
1 small garlic clove, minced
½ cup finely grated pecorino cheese (about 2 ounces), plus more for sprinkling
¼ cup plus 3 tablespoons extra-virgin olive oil, plus more for topping
2½ cups loosely packed fresh mint leaves, plus more for garnish
12 ounces angel hair pasta (capellini)
Turkey and Pancetta Meatballs (recipe follows)

Bring a small pot of water to a boil; add 1 tablespoon salt. Blanch fava beans until bright green and tender when pinched, about 2 minutes. Transfer beans with a slotted spoon to a colander and run under cold water to stop the cooking. When cool, peel off the tough outer skins, squeezing the beans from the skins (discard skins).

Pulse almonds with garlic in a food processor until coarsely ground. Add cheese and the oil; process to a coarse paste. Add mint, and pulse a few times until coarsely chopped. Season with salt and pepper. Transfer to a small bowl and top with a thin layer to preserve the color.

Bring a large pot of water to a boil; add 2 tablespoons salt. Cook pasta until al dente according to package instructions (about 4 minutes for dried, 1 minute for fresh); reserve ½ cup cooking water, then drain pasta. In a warmed serving bowl, mix pesto with enough reserved cooking water to form a thin sauce. Add pasta and fava beans, and toss well to combine.

To serve, divide pasta among four dishes, and top with meatballs; garnish with mint, and sprinkle with more cheese.

{ This meal is classic Italian comfort food at its best: simple to prepare yet complex in flavor, satisfying without being too filling. Serve with a light-bodied red wine with some earthiness, such as Dolcetto d'Alba or barbera, or a crisp white wine from Friuli, such as pinot grigio or Tocai Friulano.

Turkey and Pancetta Meatballs

Turkey meatballs are a leaner alternative to those made with ground beef. These are flecked with sage and lemon zest; pancetta adds flavor and keeps them from drying out. Serves 4

  1 pound ground turkey, preferably 7% fat
  1 ounce thinly sliced pancetta, finely chopped (¼ cup)
  ½ onion, finely chopped (about ¾ cup)
  1 garlic clove, minced
  ¾ cup fresh fine bread crumbs (see page 260)
    Coarse salt and freshly ground pepper
  1 large whole egg plus 1 large egg yolk
  1 tablespoon finely chopped fresh sage
  1 teaspoon finely grated lemon zest
    Olive oil, for frying

Gently mix turkey, pancetta, onion, garlic, and bread crumbs in a large bowl; season with 1 teaspoon salt and a pinch of pepper. Stir in the egg and yolk, sage, and zest. Form mixture into 1-inch meatballs.

Heat 1 to 2 tablespoons oil in a large heavy skillet over medium-high until hot but not smoking. Cook the meatballs in a single layer (work in two batches, if necessary), turning as needed, until browned on all sides and cooked through, about 7 minutes. Transfer to a plate and tent with parchment paper, then foil, to keep warm.

Spring Salad with Fresh Mozzarella

This salad is very simple, so the quality of each ingredient is key. Use the best olive oil and sea salt you can find, and look for fresh mozzarella made from buffalo milk, which has a wonderful tangy taste; the cheese is often sold in bulk or packaged in water at cheese shops, gourmet markets, and Italian grocers. Other fresh mozzarella (made from cow's milk), including bocconcini, can be substituted. Serves 4

  2½ cups mâche (2 to 3 packages) or tender baby lettuce leaves
   1 ball (10 ounces) fresh buffalo mozzarella, halved lengthwise, sliced ½ inch thick crosswise
   2 scallions, white and pale-green parts only, trimmed and thinly sliced
   4 radishes, trimmed and sliced into rounds
     Coarse salt and freshly ground pepper
   2 tablespoons extra-virgin olive oil

Place mâche on a platter, and arrange mozzarella and radishes on top. Sprinkle with scallions. Just before serving, season with salt and pepper, and drizzle with the oil.

When deciding on a salad course, consider a range of texture: tender lettuce, creamy mozzarella, and crisp radishes combine in a lively dish "dressed" only with extra-virgin olive oil.

Coffee Ice Cream Affogato

The word affogato *means "drowned" in Italian; affogato al caffè is the name of a popular dessert in which hot espresso is poured over gelato. The bitterness of the espresso acts as a pleasant counterpoint to the sweet creaminess of the ice cream; liqueur intensifies the overall flavor. Although traditional gelato is denser than ice cream and therefore melts more slowly, you can use either one for equally delicious results. If you prefer, substitute very strong brewed coffee for the espresso.*
Serves 4

- 1 pint best-quality coffee gelato or ice cream
- 4 ounces liqueur, such as sambuca, amaretto, or Frangelico (optional)
- 4 demitasse cups freshly brewed espresso

Just before serving, scoop gelato into four small bowls or large coffee cups. Divide liqueur among four small glasses, if using; serve liqueur and espresso alongside each bowl for guests to pour over the gelato.

How to Make Espresso

Producing a great cup of espresso at home depends on the quality of the beans used and how they are brewed. In a professional-grade espresso machine, hot water (between 190°F and 200°F) is shot through tightly packed grounds at very high pressure. The pressure produces the frothy topping, called "crema," that's distinctive of an excellent cup of espresso. Although there are a variety of espresso makers designed for the home, in a wide range of prices, most of these machines (and the traditional Italian stove-top conical makers) don't have the pressure to create the crema, but it's still possible to produce a flavorful shot. Make sure to buy espresso beans from a shop with high turnover, and preferably one that roasts its own beans. The beans should be ground to an even texture resembling that of granulated sugar. (If the grounds are too coarse, water will pass through them without extracting enough flavor; too fine, and they may clog your machine.) Use 1 tablespoon of espresso for every ounce of water and, for the best flavor, never let a fresh cup sit for more than a few minutes.

A seemingly impromptu dessert is as easy as one-two-three: Scoop some gelato or ice cream into bowls or mugs, then give each guest a cup of freshly brewed espresso and a shot of liqueur—sambuca is shown here—for pouring over the top. Offer more sambuca for sipping with the dessert.

Roast Salmon and Potatoes
Mustard-Herb Butter
Haricots Verts with Tapenade
Lemon Mousse

PREPARATION SCHEDULE

1. Make mousse, and chill.

2. Begin roasting potatoes; add salmon to pan, and continue roasting.

3. Whip cream and fold into mousse; chill.

4. Cook haricots verts; toss with tapenade.

5. Spread mustard-herb butter on salmon and potatoes.

Roast Salmon and Potatoes

You can use small Yukon Gold potatoes in place of the finger-lings; halve or quarter them to make uniform pieces. Serves 4

- 1 tablespoon plus 2 teaspoons extra-virgin olive oil, plus more for pan
- 1 pound fingerling potatoes, halved lengthwise
  Coarse salt and freshly ground pepper
- 1 fillet (2 pounds) salmon, preferably wild, skin on
  Mustard-Herb Butter
  Fresh herbs, plus more leaves for garnish

Preheat oven to 400°F. Brush the bottom of a roasting pan with oil. Place potatoes in pan; season with ¾ teaspoon salt and a pinch of pepper, and drizzle with 1 tablespoon oil. Toss to coat, and spread in a single layer. Roast 30 minutes, turning with a spatula after potatoes begin to turn golden underneath (about 20 minutes).

Season salmon on both sides with salt and pepper. Push potatoes to edges of pan, and place salmon, skin side down, in center of pan. Brush with remaining 2 teaspoons oil, and roast until salmon barely flakes on the edges when pressed, 25 to 28 minutes for medium-rare (it will still be pink in the center). Brush salmon and potatoes with herb butter while still hot. Serve, garnished with herbs.

Mustard-Herb Butter

This versatile compound butter goes well with any roasted, grilled, or broiled fish, chicken, or pork dish. It can also be stirred into cooked rice or chilled and sliced for topping baked potatoes. The recipe calls for a combination of parsley, thyme, and chervil, but you can vary the herbs to suit your tastes; small-leaf herbs like these can be left whole, but those with larger leaves, such as basil, should be chopped. Makes about ½ cup

- ½ cup (1 stick) unsalted butter, room temperature
- 1 tablespoon Dijon mustard
- ¼ cup tightly packed small herb leaves, such as parsley, thyme, and chervil, plus more leaves for garnish
  Coarse salt and freshly ground pepper

Stir butter and mustard together in a small bowl until smooth. Stir in the herbs and season with ¼ teaspoon salt and ⅛ teaspoon pepper, or to taste. (The compound butter can be made ahead, rolled tightly in parchment paper to form a log, and then wrapped in plastic; store in the refrigerator up to 1 week, or in the freezer up to 1 month.)

{ Take a few ingredients and some flavorful seasonings, cook them by simple methods, and you have the makings of an almost effortless meal. Here the salmon and potatoes are roasted in one pan, then brushed with a flavored butter to finish.

Haricots Verts with Tapenade

Green beans are a fine substitute for haricots verts; just be sure to trim the ends and remove the strings before cooking. Look for jars of tapenade—a seasoned olive paste—at cheese shops and many supermarkets. Serves 4

    Coarse salt and freshly ground pepper
¾ pound haricots verts
2 tablespoons black-olive tapenade
1 teaspoon extra-virgin olive oil

Bring a medium pot of water to a boil, then add 1 tablespoon salt. Blanch haricots verts until bright and crisp-tender, about 2 minutes. Use a slotted spoon or a mesh spider to transfer beans to a large bowl.

Toss with tapenade and stir in oil while still warm, then season with salt and pepper.

Lemon Mousse

Made with just four kitchen staples, the mousse is likely to become a favorite standby dessert (just be sure to allow enough time for proper chilling). Serves 4

4 large eggs
⅔ cup sugar
⅔ cup fresh lemon juice (from 2 to 3 lemons)
1 cup heavy cream, well chilled

Stir together eggs, sugar, and lemon juice in a medium saucepan. Cook over medium-low heat, stirring constantly with a wooden spoon, until slightly thickened, about 2 minutes. Raise heat to medium; continue to cook, stirring constantly, until mixture is thick enough to coat the back of the spoon, about 5 minutes. Strain through a fine sieve, pressing with a flexible spatula, into a metal bowl. Cover with waxed paper or plastic wrap, pressing it directly on the surface of the mixture; refrigerate until well chilled, 40 to 45 minutes.

Whisk heavy cream in a metal bowl until soft peaks form. Gently fold cream into lemon mixture with a flexible spatula. Cover tightly with plastic wrap, and refrigerate at least 30 minutes (or up to 2 days) before spooning into dessert cups.

Any lemon dessert is always a lovely way to cap off a meal; this creamy mousse is at once luxurious and spare, its pure eggshell color belying the richness of the dish. Porcelain teacups in the same creamy shade as the dessert are set on a matching platter for easy serving.

{ For a fast alternative to traditional corned beef and cabbage, serve roast beef and quick-braised cabbage instead; cream scones and a glass of Irish beer round out a meal fit for Saint Patrick's Day (or no special occasion at all).

Roast Beef with Horseradish Sauce
Green Cabbage with Leek
Currant Scones
Baked Cinnamon Apples

PREPARATION SCHEDULE	1. Brown beef, then roast in oven.	2. Meanwhile, make dough for scones, and arrange on baking sheet.	3. Remove beef from oven; raise oven temperature, and bake scones.	4. Braise cabbage, and make horseradish sauce.	5. Bake apples just before serving.

Roast Beef with Horseradish Sauce

After the beef reaches 140 degrees, let it stand at room temperature for at least ten minutes before carving; it will continue to cook during this time, so be careful not to let it go too long in the oven. Resting the meat on a wire rack will keep it from becoming soggy. Serves 4

- 1 top or bottom round beef roast (about 2 pounds), tied (ask the butcher to do this for you)
  Coarse salt and freshly ground pepper
- 2 tablespoons safflower or other neutral-tasting oil
- 6 small onions, halved lengthwise
- 1 cup sour cream
- ¼ cup grated peeled fresh horseradish (or prepared horseradish)
- 1 tablespoon fresh lemon juice (from ½ lemon)

Preheat oven to 375°F. Season beef all over with salt and pepper. Heat oil in a large ovenproof sauté pan over high until hot but not smoking. Add beef; brown on all sides, about 5 minutes total. Remove from heat.

Place onion halves in pan, cut sides down. Transfer pan to oven. Cook beef and onions until an instant-read thermometer inserted into center of beef registers 140°F (for medium-rare), 35 to 40 minutes. Transfer beef to a wire rack set over a rimmed baking sheet, and let stand 10 minutes before carving. Reserve onions.

Stir together sour cream, horseradish, lemon juice, ¼ teaspoon salt, and pepper to taste in a small bowl. Serve beef with horseradish sauce and roasted onions.

Green Cabbage with Leek

Chicken stock makes a flavorful braising liquid for cabbage (no added butter or oil necessary), a bit of leek lends sweetness to the dish. Serves 4

- 3½ cups chicken stock, homemade (see page 260) or low-sodium store-bought
  Coarse salt
- 10 whole black peppercorns
- 1 dried bay leaf
- 1 small green cabbage (about 2 pounds), cut into 8 wedges and thick core removed
- 1 small leek, white and pale-green parts only, halved lengthwise and cut crosswise into ½-inch-thick pieces, washed well and drained (see page 260)
  Freshly ground pepper

Bring stock, 1 teaspoon salt, the peppercorns, and bay leaf to a boil in a medium pot over medium-high heat. Add cabbage and leek. Cover; reduce heat to medium. Simmer until cabbage is tender, 12 to 15 minutes.

Transfer cabbage and some of the broth to a serving platter, leaving bay leaf and peppercorns behind. Serve warm, sprinkled with pepper.

Currant Scones

Overworking the dough will make the scones tough, so handle it as little as possible. The dough should come together into a rough mound and feel slightly sticky. Makes 8

- 1¾ cups all-purpose flour, plus more for dusting
- ¼ cup wheat germ
- 3 tablespoons sugar
- 1 tablespoon baking powder
- ½ teaspoon coarse salt
- ⅓ cup dried currants
- 1¼ cups heavy cream
- 2 tablespoons unsalted butter, melted, plus more, softened, for serving

Preheat oven to 425°F. Whisk together flour, wheat germ, sugar, baking powder, and salt in a large bowl. Stir in currants. Add cream, and stir just until combined.

Turn out dough onto a lightly floured work surface. Gently gather dough into a mound just until it holds together. Pat into an 8-inch disk (about ½ inch thick). With a bench scraper, cut into 8 equal wedges.

Arrange wedges on a baking sheet lined with parchment. Brush tops with the melted butter. Bake, rotating sheet halfway through, until golden brown, about 20 minutes. Transfer scones to a wire rack, and let cool. Serve warm or at room temperature, with softened butter.

Baked Cinnamon Apples

Using cinnamon sticks in addition to ground cinnamon intensifies the flavor of the spice. Serve the apples with vanilla ice cream, if desired. Serves 4

- 4 tablespoons (½ stick) unsalted butter
- ¼ cup sugar
- ½ teaspoon ground cinnamon
- 4 whole cinnamon sticks
- 4 small Granny Smith apples (unpeeled), halved lengthwise, seeds and stems left intact

Preheat oven to 350°F. Melt butter in a large ovenproof skillet over medium heat. Stir in sugar and ground cinnamon, and add cinnamon sticks. Arrange apples in skillet, cut sides down.

Transfer skillet to oven. Bake apples until tender, about 12 minutes. Place 2 apple halves in each serving dish, cut sides up, and drizzle evenly with butter mixture from skillet. Garnish with the cinnamon sticks. Serve warm.

A wood block makes a striking pedestal for dessert. Apple-green linen napkins emulate the color of the fresh fruit. Cinnamon sticks, baked alongside, do double duty as flavor enhancer and garnish.

Boneless lamb steak is a quick-cooking alternative to larger roasts, especially when cut into cubes and cooked in a hot grill pan. Mint, a classic partner for lamb, flavors the marinade. The accompaniments—pita bread, artichokes, and olives—are in-spired by Mediterranean cooking, as is the citrus dessert.

Crudités with Dill Butter
Herbed Lamb and Pita
Artichokes and Olives in White Wine
Greek Yogurt with Clementines
and Pistachios

PREPARATION SCHEDULE

1. Prepare herb rub for lamb.

2. Trim and halve artichokes, then braise with olives.

3. Make dill butter; trim vegetables for crudités and cover with a damp towel.

4. Warm pitas; cook lamb.

5. Assemble dessert just before serving.

Herbed Lamb and Pita

For this recipe, an outdoor grill will work as well as a grill pan, but you will need to thread the meat cubes onto skewers before grilling (and remove skewers before serving). Soak wooden skewers in water for thirty minutes before grilling to keep them from scorching. Serves 4

¼ cup plus 2 tablespoons finely chopped fresh mint

2 tablespoons finely chopped fresh thyme

2 shallots, minced (about ¼ cup)

½ teaspoon ground allspice

¼ cup plus 2 tablespoons extra-virgin olive oil
Coarse salt and freshly ground pepper

4 lamb steaks (each about 7 ounces and 1 inch thick, and cut from the leg or top round)

4 small (7-inch) pita breads

Preheat oven to 375°F. Stir together mint, thyme, shallots, allspice, and oil in a bowl; add 1 tablespoon salt, and season with pepper. Reserve one-third of mixture for pita.

Cut lamb into 2-inch-long pieces. Add to bowl and toss with herb mixture; let marinate at room temperature 10 minutes (or refrigerate up to 1 hour).

Meanwhile, spread reserved herb mixture over pitas, dividing evenly. Place on a baking sheet and bake until heated through, about 5 minutes. Remove from oven; tent with parchment paper, then foil, to keep warm.

Heat a grill pan over medium-high. Working in two batches to avoid crowding pan, grill lamb until seared on the first side (the cubes should release easily from the

pan), about 2 minutes, then continue cooking and turning until all sides are browned, about 4 minutes more. Transfer each batch to a platter and tent with parchment, then foil, to keep warm. Serve lamb with pitas.

Crudités with Dill Butter

Use carrots and radishes of different colors and varieties, keeping the tops on if desired. Sea salt, such as Maldon, adds brighter flavor than regular coarse salt, but either can be used in the dill butter. Serves 4

½ cup (1 stick) unsalted butter, room temperature
1 tablespoon plus 1 teaspoon finely chopped fresh dill
1 teaspoon coarse salt, preferably sea salt (such as Maldon)
8 to 12 small carrots (about ½ pound), peeled and halved lengthwise if large
8 to 12 radishes (about ½ pound), trimmed

Mix butter with dill and salt until completely incorporated; transfer to a small crock or ramekin for serving. Arrange the vegetables on a platter and place butter alongside for dipping.

Artichokes and Olives in White Wine

Artichokes will quickly discolor once they are trimmed and exposed to air, so work with one at a time, and soak them in lemon (acidulated) water until ready to cook. Serves 4

2 lemons, halved
4 medium artichokes (about 10 ounces each)
3 tablespoons extra-virgin olive oil
2 garlic cloves, crushed with the side of a large knife
½ cup dry white wine
¾ cup water
½ cup green olives, rinsed
6 thyme sprigs
1 teaspoon coarse salt

Squeeze 2 lemon halves into a medium bowl of water, then drop in halves. Working with one artichoke at a time, remove outer leaves until pale green leaves are exposed; cut off top two-thirds of leaves (where the darker part begins) with a serrated or large chef's knife. Trim away dark green exterior layer of base and stalks with a paring knife. Cut each artichoke in half lengthwise through heart, and use a small spoon to scoop out sharp inner leaves and choke. As you work, immediately drop artichoke halves into lemon water to prevent discoloration.

Squeeze juice from remaining lemon (about ¼ cup), and combine with all other ingredients in a medium, deep-sided sauté pan, stirring to combine. Add artichokes, cut sides down, in pan. Cover and bring to a rapid simmer over medium-high heat, about 2 minutes; reduce heat to medium, and simmer until artichokes are tender (but not falling apart) when pierced with a fork, 15 to 20 minutes.

Use a slotted spoon to lift artichokes and olives from the pan and divide among four plates, then spoon a bit of broth over each, just to moisten.

Greek Yogurt with Clementines and Pistachios

Add a drizzle of honey for extra sweetness, if desired. Serves 4

1 container (about 16 ounces) Greek-style plain yogurt
3 clementines or tangerines, peeled and segmented
¼ cup shelled unsalted pistachios, coarsely chopped

Spoon yogurt into four dessert bowls, dividing evenly, and top each portion with 3 or 4 fruit segments. Sprinkle with pistachios, and serve extra segments on the side.

{ Sweet as candy and intensely flavored, clementines are perfect for dessert on their own, but they are even more irresistible served with tangy yogurt and chopped nuts for creamy-crunchy contrast. Glass tumblers show off the colors.

Asparagus-Parmesan Tart
Shrimp in Saffron Broth
Couscous with Golden Raisins
Apricot-Almond Ice Cream Sandwiches

PREPARATION SCHEDULE

1. Prepare apricots and fold into ice cream; freeze.

2. Form tart shell and chill.

3. Meanwhile, cook couscous; assemble and bake tart.

4. Cook broth and shrimp.

5. Assemble ice cream sandwiches.

Shrimp in Saffron Broth

Saffron is found at specialty food stores and many supermarkets. Be sure to buy it only in threads, not powdered form; the redder the saffron, the higher the quality. Although expensive, saffron is used sparingly in recipes and, stored in a dry spot away from direct heat or sunlight, has a long shelf life. Serves 4

¼   cup extra-virgin olive oil
1   fennel bulb, trimmed and cut into ¼-inch dice (about 2 cups)
3   carrots, cut into ¼-inch dice (about 1 cup)
½   teaspoon saffron threads
1½   pounds large (21 to 25 count) shrimp, peeled and deveined (see page 260)
     Coarse salt and freshly ground pepper
½   cup dry white wine
1½   cups chicken stock, homemade (see page 260) or low-sodium store-bought
     Couscous with Golden Raisins

Heat a large sauté pan over medium. Add oil and heat until hot but not smoking. Cook fennel, carrots, and saffron until vegetables are starting to soften, stirring occasionally, about 4 minutes.

Season shrimp with salt and pepper; add to pan and cook 1 minute, then turn shrimp. Pour in wine and stock, and cook just until shrimp are pink and opaque throughout, about 2 minutes.

Serve shrimp, vegetables, and broth over couscous in shallow bowls.

Couscous with Golden Raisins

Israeli couscous has larger granules and a chewier texture than the regular variety. Look for it at health-food stores, Middle Eastern shops, and many supermarkets. Toasting the couscous before adding liquid gives it a nutty taste. This dish is delicious hot or at room temperature; if serving at room temperature, stir in a tablespoon of extra-virgin olive oil at the end, instead of butter. Serves 4

1   tablespoon extra-virgin olive oil
1½   cups Israeli couscous
1¾   cups plus 2 tablespoons water
½   cup golden raisins
     Coarse salt and freshly ground pepper
1   tablespoon unsalted butter

Heat oil in a 4-quart pot over medium-high. Add couscous; stir to coat with oil and cook, stirring, until lightly toasted, 1 to 2 minutes.

Add the water and raisins; season with salt and pepper. Bring to a boil, then reduce heat to medium-low. Cover and simmer until couscous is tender and has absorbed the liquid, 8 to 10 minutes. Remove from heat. Fluff with a fork and stir in butter before serving.

{ Store-bought puff pastry makes easy work of the starter for this meal—a shaved-asparagus and parmesan tart. It's followed by seared shrimp and tender couscous, each of which takes mere minutes to cook. Antique etched wineglasses, along with aqua-rimmed soup bowls and coordinating plates, are carried to the table on a linen-lined tray.

Asparagus-Parmesan Tart

For the most flavorful (and flaky) results, look for all-butter brands of frozen puff pastry, such as Dufour. Serves 4

- 1 sheet (14 ounces) frozen puff pastry, thawed
  All-purpose flour, for dusting
- 1 large egg, well beaten
- 10 medium asparagus spears, tough ends trimmed, shaved into thin strips using a vegetable peeler
- 2 teaspoons extra-virgin olive oil
  Coarse salt and freshly ground pepper
- ½ cup finely grated Parmigiano-Reggiano cheese

Preheat oven to 400°F. Roll out dough on a lightly floured work surface, just until creases are smooth. Trim dough to a 10-inch square. Lightly score a ½-inch border around dough. Brush off excess flour and transfer dough to a parchment-lined baking sheet. Freeze 15 minutes.

Brush border of dough with the beaten egg. Bake until puffed and starting to brown, 10 to 12 minutes. Toss asparagus with the oil, and season with salt and pepper.

Remove tart shell from oven and press down on the center with a spatula. Arrange asparagus on top. Bake until asparagus is crisp-tender, about 8 minutes. Remove from oven and sprinkle cheese evenly on top. Bake until cheese is melted, about 4 minutes more. Let cool on a wire rack 5 minutes before slicing into squares.

Apricot-Almond Ice Cream Sandwiches

Belgian almond-butter thins (such as those made by Jules Destrooper) are very thin and crisp and rectangular in shape; look for them at supermarkets and specialty food stores. You can substitute other almond wafers or thin ginger cookies. Makes 8 to 12

- ¼ cup warm brandy
- 1 cup dried apricots, finely chopped (½ cup)
- 2 tablespoons apricot jam
  Unsalted butter, for baking dish
- 1 pint vanilla ice cream, softened
- 16 to 24 almond-butter thins

In a bowl, pour brandy over apricots; let sit 1 minute, then stir in jam to combine. Refrigerate 5 minutes.

Butter an 8-inch square baking dish. Line with parchment paper, leaving a 4-inch overhang. Fold the apricot mixture into ice cream, then spread into the prepared dish. Fold parchment over ice cream to cover completely; freeze until firm, about 50 minutes.

To assemble, cut the ice cream into pieces to match the cookies, and layer to form sandwiches. (The sandwiches can be wrapped tightly in plastic and frozen up to 1 week.)

Ice cream sandwiches are a nostalgic treat any time of year; made with store-bought almond wafers and vanilla ice cream blended with brandy-soaked apricots, they are a fanciful yet foolproof dessert for entertaining.

Strip Steak with Chimichurri
Roasted Potato Wedges
Sautéed Spinach and Vidalia Onion
Torrijas

PREPARATION SCHEDULE

1. Roast potatoes.

2. Meanwhile, make chimichurri sauce.

3. Grill steaks; let rest.

4. Sauté spinach and onion.

5. Cook dessert just before serving.

Strip Steak with Chimichurri

New York strip steak is also known by other names, including shell steak, Delmonico, and Kansas City strip steak. Serves 4

- ½ cup minced red onion (about ½ onion)
- ⅓ cup coarsely chopped fresh flat-leaf parsley
- 1 tablespoon coarsely chopped fresh oregano
- 1 tablespoon minced garlic
- ⅓ cup extra-virgin olive oil
- 3 tablespoons red wine vinegar
- ½ teaspoon crushed red-pepper flakes
- 1 tablespoon finely grated lemon zest
  Coarse salt and freshly ground black pepper
- 2 New York strip steaks (each about 1 pound and 1 inch thick)

Mix all the ingredients except the steaks in a bowl, seasoning with 2½ teaspoons salt and ½ teaspoon black pepper; let stand at room temperature, about 15 minutes.

Pat dry steaks with paper towels, and season both sides with salt and pepper. Place in a large cast-iron skillet (avoid crowding). Cook over medium-high heat until browned and a crust has formed on the bottom, about 4 minutes. Turn steaks and continue cooking about 2 minutes more, depending on thickness, for medium rare.

Transfer steaks to a cutting board and let rest 10 minutes. To serve, slice crosswise (against the grain) into ¼- to ½-inch-thick pieces. Divide steak among four plates and spoon about 1 tablespoon sauce on top of each. Pass remaining sauce on the side.

Sautéed Spinach and Vidalia Onion

Vidalia onion adds a touch of sweetness to offset the mildly bitter taste of the spinach. If you can't find Vidalia, use a sweet yellow onion instead. Regular spinach can also be used instead of baby spinach; trim the tough stems before cooking. If necessary, to avoid overfilling the pan, add the spinach in batches, tossing until each wilts before adding the next. Serves 4

- 2 tablespoons olive oil
- 1 Vidalia onion, thinly sliced
- 1 pound baby spinach, washed well and drained
  Coarse salt and freshly ground pepper

Heat oil in a large sauté pan over medium-high. Cook onion, stirring occasionally, until softened, about 5 minutes. Add the spinach. Cook, tossing constantly to cook evenly, until wilted. Season with salt and pepper, and serve immediately.

{ Nearly every culture has a version of steak and potatoes, and this one is borrowed from Argentina, where chimichurri—a piquant blend of garlic, vinegar, lemon juice, chile flakes, and herbs—is the national condiment. Serving the meal family-style (the sliced steak and potato wedges are on mid-century ceramic dishes from Russel Wright) sets a relaxed mood.

Roasted Potato Wedges

The potatoes are delicious with a bit of chimichurri sauce drizzled over the top. Add more garlic to the potatoes if you prefer a stronger flavor. Serves 4

3 russet potatoes (2 pounds)
1 tablespoon minced garlic, or to taste
3 tablespoons olive oil
   Coarse salt and freshly ground pepper

Preheat oven to 450°F. Cut each potato lengthwise into 12 wedges. Toss potatoes with garlic and oil on a rimmed baking sheet, then season with salt and pepper. Spread in an even layer.

Roast until browned and crisp on the bottom, about 25 minutes; turn wedges with a spatula and continue cooking until browned and crisp all over, about 20 minutes more.

Torrijas

This supremely easy sweet pressed toast is a traditional dessert in Spain, where it is also sometimes served for breakfast. Serves 4

½ cup sweetened condensed milk, plus more for drizzling (optional)
1 loaf soft white French bread (12 inches long and 4 inches wide), split lengthwise and then cut crosswise (to form 4 pieces)
2 tablespoons unsalted butter

Spoon 2 tablespoons condensed milk on the cut side of each piece of bread, spreading it evenly with the back of the spoon. Melt 1 tablespoon butter in a large heavy-bottom skillet over medium-high heat.

When the butter starts to sizzle, place the bread, milk side down, in the pan; reduce heat to medium-low. Place a smaller skillet weighted with a canned good on top of bread and cook until deep golden and slightly crisp, about 3 minutes (it should be pressed to ¼ to ½ inch thick). Flip bread with a spatula and reduce heat to low; continue cooking, pressed and weighted, until heated through, about 2 minutes more.

Transfer bread to a cutting board and cut into 2-inch-wide triangles or squares. Serve warm, drizzled with more condensed milk, if desired.

A batter-free, quicker version of *torrijas* (Spanish-style French toast) is made by brushing bread with sweetened condensed milk, then cooking in butter, while pressing with a weight, until crisp. Serve with strong coffee (dunking encouraged).

Tomato, Rice, and Sausage Soup
Catfish Po'boys
Tangy Coleslaw
Bananas with Caramel Sauce

PREPARATION SCHEDULE

1. Toss together slaw; cover and refrigerate.

2. Cook soup.

3. Meanwhile, make caramel sauce.

4. Fry fish; assemble po'boys.

5. Slice bananas and assemble dessert just before serving.

Catfish Po'boys

Look for catfish that is moist, not spongy or dry. Serves 4

    Peanut oil, for frying
¼ cup plus 2 tablespoons mayonnaise
¼ cup plus 2 tablespoons whole-grain mustard
1¼ pounds catfish fillets
    Coarse salt and freshly ground black pepper
¼ teaspoon cayenne pepper
½ cup buttermilk
1 cup cornmeal
1 cup all-purpose flour
2 soft (14-inch-long) baguettes, split and halved (or 4 sandwich rolls, such as hoagie or hero rolls)
¼ head iceberg lettuce, leaves separated

Heat 3 inches oil in a heavy-bottom pot over medium-high until it registers 350°F on a deep-fry thermometer. Mix mayonnaise and mustard in a small bowl.

Pat dry catfish with paper towels, and season with salt, black pepper, and cayenne. Slice lengthwise down the middle, then crosswise into ½-inch strips. Toss with buttermilk. Whisk cornmeal and flour with 1 teaspoon salt and a pinch of black pepper in another bowl.

Working in batches, lift fish from buttermilk, letting excess drip back into bowl; dredge in cornmeal mixture, shaking off excess. Gently lower pieces into oil with a mesh spider or slotted spoon; cook until golden, about 5 minutes. Transfer to paper towels to drain; season with salt.

Spread each roll with some mayonnaise mixture. Divide fish pieces evenly among rolls, top with lettuce, and serve with extra mayonnaise on the side.

Tangy Coleslaw

Unlike classic American-style coleslaw, this one is bound with mustard, vinegar, and oil instead of mayonnaise. Serves 4

1 head green cabbage (1 pound), halved lengthwise, core removed
1 small red onion, halved lengthwise, then thinly sliced crosswise
1 tablespoon sugar
1 tablespoon Dijon mustard
¼ cup apple cider vinegar
2 tablespoons safflower or other neutral-tasting oil
1 teaspoon coarse salt

Using a mandoline or a very sharp knife, slice the cabbage as thin as possible. Place in a bowl and toss with remaining ingredients until cabbage is thoroughly coated.

Cover with plastic wrap; refrigerate at least 45 minutes (or up to 3 hours) to allow flavors to meld. Toss again just before serving.

{ A cup of soup and hearty sandwich make a meal that is equal parts comfort and fun. Po'boys are a New Orleans specialty, whether made with catfish, as in this menu, or oysters. Brown kraft paper, vintage condiment cups, and glasses of cold beer lend the table authentic fish-shack appeal.

Bananas with Caramel Sauce

For a pretty presentation, slice the bananas on the diagonal or at oblique angles (alternating slices at forty-five-degree angles in opposite directions). Avoid stirring the caramel once the sugar has melted, as this can cause crystals to form, which will ruin the texture. Crème fraîche is available at many supermarkets and specialty stores; or you can whip a quarter cup of heavy cream to stiff peaks and use in its place. Serves 4

  1 cup sugar
  ½ cup water
  ¾ cup heavy cream
  4 slightly underripe bananas
  ¼ cup crème fraîche
  ½ cup pecan halves, lightly toasted (see page 260)

Cook sugar and the water in a medium heavy-bottom saucepan over medium heat, gently stirring occasionally, until sugar has dissolved and syrup is clear. Continue cooking, without stirring, until the syrup comes to a boil, washing down sides of pan with a wet pastry brush two or three times to prevent crystals from forming. Let boil, gently swirling pan occasionally, until syrup is medium amber in color. Carefully pour heavy cream down the side of the pan (it will spatter) and stir until smooth. Remove from heat; cover to keep warm, up to 1 hour.

When ready to serve, cut bananas into 1-inch pieces. Divide among four dishes, and drizzle with caramel (gently reheated if necessary). Stir crème fraîche to soften, then dollop 1 tablespoon onto each portion, and sprinkle with pecans.

Tomato, Rice, and Sausage Soup

Andouille sausage is a specialty of Cajun cooking; kielbasa is a good (and less spicy) substitute. Serves 4

  1 tablespoon safflower or other neutral-tasting oil
  5 ounces andouille sausage, one-quarter cut into small dice, the rest into ¼-inch-thick half-moons
  ½ red bell pepper, ribs and seeds removed, minced
  ½ yellow onion, minced
  2 celery stalks, minced
  1 garlic clove, thinly sliced
  1 teaspoon fresh thyme leaves
  1 cup canned whole peeled tomatoes, pureed
  4 cups chicken stock, homemade (see page 260) or low-sodium store-bought
  ½ cup long-grain white rice
  ½ teaspoon apple cider or distilled white vinegar
      Coarse salt and freshly ground pepper

Heat oil in a 4-quart saucepan over medium-high until hot but not smoking. Cook sausage, stirring occasionally, until browned, 3 to 5 minutes. Add bell pepper, onion, celery, garlic, and thyme. Cook over medium-low, stirring occasionally, 10 minutes.

Add tomatoes, stock, and rice; bring to a boil. Reduce heat and simmer until rice is plump, about 20 minutes. Remove from heat. Stir in vinegar, and season with salt and pepper.

{ In this easy take on bananas Foster, another New Orleans creation, bananas are sliced and drizzled with caramel sauce (rather than being sautéed with butter and brown sugar). Crème fraîche stands in for the traditional ice cream; toasted pecans add flavor and crunch. A fine aged rum is served alongside for sipping.

Coconut Poached Chicken
Crisp Rice-Noodle Cakes
Watercress with Garlic-Chile Oil
Minty Green Tea Milkshakes

PREPARATION SCHEDULE

1. Cook the noodles, and drain well.
2. Poach the chicken; reduce poaching liquid.
3. Form and pan-fry noodle cakes.
4. Heat garlic-chile oil, then toss with watercress.
5. Blend milkshakes just before serving.

Coconut Poached Chicken

Be sure to buy only unsweetened coconut milk, not cream of coconut or the type usually used for making cocktails (such as Coco López), and shake the can vigorously before opening. Serves 4

- 2 cans (14 ounces each) unsweetened coconut milk
- 2 pounds skinless, bone-in chicken breasts
- 1 piece (about 1 inch) fresh ginger, peeled and sliced into ¼-inch rounds
- 2 garlic cloves, smashed with the side of a large knife
- 1 scallion, trimmed and cut into 2-inch pieces
  Coarse salt
- 1 teaspoon Asian fish sauce (such as *nam pla*)
- 1 teaspoon fresh lime juice

Combine coconut milk, chicken, ginger, garlic, scallion, and ¼ teaspoon salt in a 4-quart saucepan. Bring just to a boil over medium-high heat, then reduce heat to medium; simmer until juices run clear when chicken is pierced, 15 to 18 minutes (an instant-read thermometer inserted in thickest part, avoiding the bone, should register 160°F). Transfer chicken to a platter.

Raise heat to medium-high. Cook until poaching liquid is reduced by half, 3 to 4 minutes. Strain liquid through a fine sieve into a heatproof bowl (discard solids); stir in fish sauce and lime juice.

Remove the chicken meat from the bone in one piece, then slice across the grain into 1-inch-thick pieces. Divide among four plates; drizzle with some sauce, and serve the rest alongside for dipping.

Watercress with Garlic-Chile Oil

If you are unable to find serrano chiles, use a small jalapeño instead. Crushed red-pepper flakes work well, too; use a quarter of a teaspoon, or more to taste, in place of the chile. Serves 4

- 1½ bunches watercress, thick stems removed
- 3 tablespoons safflower or other neutral-tasting oil
- 1 serrano chile, quartered lengthwise (ribs and seeds removed for less heat, if desired)
- 1 garlic clove, thinly sliced
- 1 teaspoon fresh lime juice
  Coarse salt

Place the watercress in a large salad bowl. Heat oil, chile, and garlic in a small skillet over medium. When the garlic starts to turn golden brown, pour hot mixture over the watercress. Add lime juice, and season with salt; toss to coat, and serve immediately.

{ This Vietnamese-style meal presents a study in contrasts, both in texture—tender chicken, crisp noodle cake, and wilted watercress—and in flavors, with ginger, garlic, and lime in each bite, punctuated with a bit of spicy heat from the greens. A savory coconut-milk sauce is just right for dipping. Milky green jadeite plates and a brightly patterned table runner provide colorful backdrops.

Crisp Rice-Noodle Cakes

Look for soybean sprouts at Asian markets or health-food stores; mung bean sprouts are a good alternative and can be found at supermarkets, in the produce section. Makes 4

3 ounces (¼ package) rice vermicelli (or angel hair pasta)
3 ounces soybean sprouts (1½ cups)
1 tablespoon minced peeled fresh ginger
3 scallions, trimmed and sliced very thin (⅓ cup)
2 large eggs plus 1 egg white, beaten
¾ teaspoon coarse salt
¼ cup safflower or other neutral-tasting oil

Cook noodles until tender according to package instructions; drain and rinse under cool running water, then drain well. Mix noodles, sprouts, ginger, scallions, beaten eggs, and salt in a bowl to combine.

Heat oil in a large skillet over medium until hot but not smoking. Divide noodle mixture into four equal portions (about ¾ cup each). Place in pan, gently pressing to flatten. Cook until golden brown underneath, 6 to 7 minutes. Flip cakes; cook until golden on other side, 5 to 6 minutes. Turn out cakes onto a paper towel–lined plate. Blot tops with more paper towels before serving.

Minty Green Tea Milkshakes

Green tea ice cream, made with regular or soy milk, can be found at Asian food shops, natural-food stores, and many supermarkets. Makes 4

4 cups green tea ice cream (two 1-pint containers)
¾ cup plus 2 tablespoons milk
1 cup loosely packed fresh mint leaves

Puree ingredients in a blender on high speed until smooth. Divide among four tall glasses and serve immediately.

Inspired by
smoothies and
shakes popular in
many Asian coun-
tries (including
Vietnam and Thai-
land), this mint-
speckled milkshake
is a refreshing
dessert that can
be prepared in a
minute or two,
then slowly sipped
through a straw.

Pasta Shards with Fresh Herbs
Poached Eggs with Brown Butter
Arugula and Avocado Salad
Tiramisù

PREPARATION SCHEDULE

1. Assemble tiramisù, and refrigerate.

2. Boil pasta; toast pine nuts for salad.

3. Meanwhile, brown butter, and poach eggs.

4. Assemble salad.

5. Top pasta with eggs; serve.

Pasta Shards with Fresh Herbs

Using broken lasagne noodles makes it look like you made the noodles from scratch. Look for noodles with ruffled edges, which won't stick together as easily as flat noodles; stirring the noodles in the pot while the water returns to a boil will also help. The pasta can also be served on its own, without the eggs, as a first course. Serves 4

Coarse salt and freshly ground black pepper
1 package (12 ounces) lasagne noodles, broken unevenly into 2- to 4-inch pieces
½ cup coarsely chopped fresh flat-leaf parsley
2 tablespoons finely chopped fresh chives
¼ teaspoon crushed red-pepper flakes
1 teaspoon extra-virgin olive oil
Poached Eggs with Brown Butter

Bring 8 quarts of water to a boil in a large pot; add 2 table-spoons salt. Add the pasta, stirring until the water returns to a boil; cook until al dente according to package instructions. Reserve ¼ cup cooking water, and drain pasta in a colander. Transfer to a large bowl.

Reserve some parsley and chives for garnish; add the rest to pasta along with the red-pepper flakes, oil, and reserved cooking water. Toss to combine. Season with salt and pepper; serve immediately, dividing among four pasta bowls. Top with poached eggs; garnish with reserved parsley and chives.

Poached Eggs with Brown Butter

The key to perfect poached eggs is to add them to the pan one at time. Another tip: Break each egg into a cup, then tip the cup into the simmering water before gently sliding out the egg. This helps ensure that the yolk is surrounded evenly by the white. Serves 4

Coarse salt and freshly ground pepper
6 tablespoons (¾ stick) unsalted butter
8 large eggs

Bring a large shallow saucepan of water to a simmer, then add salt. Meanwhile, melt butter in a 10-inch skillet over medium heat, swirling constantly, until nut brown in color but not burnt, 3 to 4 minutes. Turn off heat.

Poach eggs in two batches: Working with one egg at a time, crack egg into a cup, and gently slide egg into water. Cook the eggs until whites are just set, 2 to 3 minutes. Using a slotted spoon, transfer eggs to paper towels to blot dry. Repeat with remaining 4 eggs. (If desired, trim away rough edges with kitchen shears.)

To serve, season with salt and pepper, and carefully place eggs in the brown butter to warm through, about 1 minute, spooning butter over the eggs. Gently place 2 eggs on top of each portion of pasta; spoon more butter over eggs.

{ The perfect midnight supper: Broken lasagne noodles flecked with fresh parsley and chives make a tender bed for poached eggs in brown butter; the soft-cooked yolks spill out to form a luscious "sauce," ideal for sopping up with rustic bread. Follow with an arugula salad and make-ahead dessert, and pour a crisp Italian white wine, such as Vermentino or pinot grigio.

Each component of this multi-textured salad delivers, including creamy avocado and crunchy pine nuts. In the Italian tradition, the salad is served as *secondi*, or second course, to follow the pasta.

Arugula and Avocado Salad

The easiest way to cut the carrots into thin strips is to halve them lengthwise and cut into three-inch lengths, then slice lengthwise into quarter-inch-wide pieces. Serves 4

- 3 tablespoons extra-virgin olive oil
- ¼ cup pine nuts
- 1 tablespoon red wine vinegar
- 1 teaspoon fresh lemon juice
- 2 ounces arugula, tough ends trimmed and washed well
- 1 to 2 carrots, cut into ¼-inch-by-3-inch pieces
- ¼ small red onion, thinly sliced
  Coarse salt
- 1 ripe but firm avocado, peeled, pitted, and thinly sliced
- 1 ounce Parmigiano-Reggiano cheese, shaved with a vegetable peeler

Combine oil and pine nuts in a medium skillet and cook over medium heat, tossing occasionally, until nuts are golden brown, about 4 minutes. Remove from heat; let cool at least 10 minutes. Use a small spoon to transfer pine nuts to a plate, then pour oil into a small bowl and whisk in vinegar and lemon juice.

Place arugula in a salad bowl; add carrot and onion, and season with salt. Spoon about 1 tablespoon dressing on top, and sprinkle with pine nuts; toss to combine. Divide salad evenly among four plates, layering halfway with the avocado. Drizzle with remaining dressing, dividing evenly, and top with cheese shavings. Serve immediately.

How to Make a Great Salad

The ultimate salad is balanced in flavor, appearance, and texture. The foundation of any salad is the lettuce or other greens, and here you can experiment with arugula, mâche, watercress, and fresh leaves; or you could choose a blend of lettuces, such as tender Bibb, crisp romaine, and crunchy radicchio. Then you can layer the lettuces with additional components, including other vegetables, cheese, or nuts (for example, an endive, pear, and roquefort salad that is sprinkled with toasted walnuts). Always use the freshest greens possible (leaf lettuces, in particular, are best when freshly picked), and arrange them in a way that pleases the eye, either by tossing everything together and finishing with a garnish that provides a bit of color or textural contrast, such as in the salad shown opposite, or by composing the components neatly on the plate. Many salads, especially those consisting of blanched or roasted vegetables, can be prepared in advance and then assembled and dressed just before serving. Toss the greens and other components lightly with dressing, taking care not to bruise the greens.

Tiramisù

The Italian form of ladyfingers (called savoiardi*) are only slightly sweet and fairly dry, so they are the best choice for using in this recipe. Quickly dip, rather than soak, the ladyfingers one at a time in the espresso; otherwise they will absorb too much liquid and become soggy. Serves 4*

- ¾ cup boiling water
- 3 tablespoons good-quality instant espresso powder (not instant coffee granules)
- ⅔ cup mascarpone cheese
- ⅔ cup heavy cream
- 3 tablespoons brandy
- ½ teaspoon pure vanilla extract
- ⅓ cup sugar
- 12 store-bought ladyfingers (about 6 ounces)
- 2 ounces bittersweet chocolate, shaved with a vegetable peeler

Mix the boiling water and espresso powder until dissolved. Refrigerate until cool, about 12 minutes. Meanwhile, with an electric mixer on medium speed, whisk together the mascarpone, heavy cream, brandy, vanilla, and sugar until soft peaks form.

Trim the ends of the ladyfingers so the cookies fit snugly (side by side) in an 8½-by-4½-inch loaf pan (preferably glass). Pour the espresso mixture into a shallow bowl. Briefly dip the ladyfingers one at a time in the espresso, turning to coat both sides.

Line the bottom of the pan with 6 ladyfingers. Spoon half the mascarpone mixture (about 1 cup) on top, then sprinkle evenly with half the shaved chocolate. Layer with the remaining ladyfingers and mascarpone mixture. Smooth the top with an offset or flexible spatula, then sprinkle with remaining chocolate.

Cover with plastic wrap and refrigerate until set, at least 1 hour (or up to overnight), or freeze for up to 30 minutes.

About Icebox Desserts

Tiramisù, trifles, and other icebox desserts are more about assembly than any actual cooking. Each dish takes store-bought items (cookies, sponge cake, and the like) and combines them with whipped cream and other simple components, such as the shaved chocolate used here. Tiramisù requires soaking ladyfingers in espresso, while sponge and pound cakes are often brushed with a flavorful simple syrup. You can adapt the formula to suit the season: layer strips of cake with whipped cream and berries for a summer trifle, fresh figs for fall, or poached pears for winter. Lemon or other fruit curds can stand in for the whipped cream; if desired, finish by sprinkling with toasted nuts or coconut.

It's easy to replicate this restaurant favorite at home (and up to a day ahead). Each forkful offers tangy, sweet, chocolatey flavors, plus bracing hints of brandy and espresso.

Fontina and Herb Flatbread
Prosciutto-Wrapped Pork Cutlets
Wilted Escarole
Amaretti-Ricotta Sandwiches

PREPARATION SCHEDULE

1. Bring dough for flatbread to room temperature; drain ricotta.

2. Bake flatbread; wrap pork in prosciutto.

3. Mix ricotta filling for sandwich cookies, and chill.

4. Cook pork; wilt escarole.

5. Assemble sandwich cookies just before serving.

Prosciutto-Wrapped Pork Cutlets

For added flavor, prepare the escarole (recipe follows) in the same sauté pan used to cook the pork. Serves 4

- 4 pork cutlets (each 4 ounces and ½ inch thick)
   Coarse salt and freshly ground pepper
- 8 thin slices prosciutto (6 ounces)
- 8 thin lemon rounds (from 1 lemon)
- 2 tablespoons olive oil

Season pork lightly on both sides with salt and pepper. Working with 1 cutlet at a time, lay 2 prosciutto slices, slightly overlapping, on a work surface. Place a lemon slice on the prosciutto, then the pork on top of the lemon. Top with 1 more lemon slice. Wrap prosciutto around pork, pressing edges to seal. Repeat with remaining prosciutto, lemon, and pork.

Heat oil until hot but not smoking in a large skillet over medium-high. Cook pork in a single layer until prosciutto is lightly browned and beginning to crisp on the first side, 4 to 5 minutes. Reduce heat to medium; turn pork, and continue cooking until pork is just cooked through, about 4 minutes more. Remove from pan. If not serving immediately, tent with parchment paper, then foil, to keep warm, up to 10 minutes.

Pork cutlets are a quick-cooking choice for busy midweek meals. Wrapping in prosciutto and lemon ensures the lean meat will be tender and flavorful after cooking—and allows it to stay that way until the rest of the food is ready. Escarole needs only a few minutes on the stove to become tender and delicious. Vintage glasses and linens in shades of green and yellow set the table.

Fontina and Herb Flatbread

Many supermarkets sell packaged pizza dough in the freezer or refrigerated sections, usually in half-pound balls; thaw frozen dough in the refrigerator. Or buy a quarter-pound of dough from your local pizzeria. Serves 4

4 ounces (½ ball) store-bought pizza dough (thawed if frozen)
   All-purpose flour, for dusting
2 tablespoons extra-virgin olive oil
2 tablespoons coarsely chopped fresh marjoram, oregano, or thyme
4 ounces Italian fontina cheese, thinly sliced
1 shallot, thinly sliced into rings
   Coarse salt and freshly ground pepper

Preheat oven to 400°F. Allow dough to come to room temperature, about 15 minutes. On a lightly floured work surface, roll dough to an 8-by-16-inch oblong. Transfer to a lightly floured baking sheet. Brush the top with half the oil; sprinkle evenly with herbs and then arrange cheese on top, covering completely. Scatter shallot rings over cheese, and drizzle with remaining oil. Season liberally with salt and pepper.

Bake, rotating sheet halfway through, until golden and crisp, 15 to 17 minutes. Remove from oven; let cool 5 minutes before cutting into wedges and serving.

Wilted Escarole

Before cutting into large pieces, wash the escarole in several changes of cold water, until you no longer see any grit at the bottom of the bowl (or sink). Then lift the greens from the water, and shake to remove excess water; the water left clinging to the leaves will help create the steam in the pan for wilting. Serves 4

1 tablespoon extra-virgin olive oil
2 garlic cloves, peeled and crushed with the side of a large knife
1 medium head escarole, cut into large pieces (12 cups)
   Coarse salt and freshly ground pepper
½ lemon

Heat oil and garlic in a large skillet over medium, and cook until garlic is golden, about 2 minutes. Add escarole and cook, tossing frequently, until wilted, about 3 minutes. If pan is too dry, add 1 to 2 tablespoons water. Season with salt and pepper and a squeeze of lemon juice.

Amaretti-Ricotta Sandwiches

Fresh ricotta has a richer flavor and creamier texture than the supermarket variety; look for it at specialty food stores, Italian grocers, and cheese shops. Crisp, airy amaretti cookies, such as Amaretti di Saronno, are used to make sweet, bite-size sandwiches. If you can't find them, try different types of cookies, such as gingersnaps or almond macaroons. Makes 12

½ cup ricotta cheese, preferably fresh (4 ounces)
½ teaspoon finely grated lemon zest
2 tablespoons confectioners' sugar
24 amaretti cookies, such as Amaretti di Saronno

Drain ricotta in a cheesecloth-lined sieve for 20 minutes. Stir together ricotta, lemon zest, and sugar, just to combine. (Filling can be refrigerated, covered with plastic wrap, up to 1 hour.)

Spread flat side of a cookie with 1 to 2 tablespoons ricotta mixture, then sandwich with another. Repeat with remaining cookies and ricotta mixture.

{ For an elegant and quick-assembly dessert, sandwich store-bought cookies with a sweet filling. Here, almond-flavored amaretti are filled with lemony ricotta.

{ This meal culls common ingredients from the Southern pantry to create a down-home meal. While seemingly simple, each dish has been given a special touch; for example, thyme and lemon are added to the spoonbread as well as the pan sauce for the chicken, and bacon flavors the dandelion greens. A vintage enameled metal trivet looks just right at home on the farmhouse table.

Pan-Roasted Chicken Pieces
Wilted Dandelion Greens
Lemon-Thyme Spoonbread
Raspberries with Honey and Buttermilk

PREPARATION SCHEDULE

1. Mix and bake spoonbread.

2. Raise oven temperature and roast chicken.

3. Make pan sauce for chicken.

4. Prepare dressing; toss with dandelion greens.

5. Assemble dessert just before serving.

Pan-Roasted Chicken Pieces

Roasting the parts takes much less time than cooking a whole chicken; each piece is seared until crisp on the stove and then finished in a very hot oven. Serves 4

- 4 bone-in, skin-on chicken drumsticks (1½ pounds)
- 4 bone-in, skin-on chicken thighs (1¼ pounds)
- 2 bone-in, skin-on chicken breasts (¾ pound)
  Coarse salt and freshly ground pepper
- 3 tablespoons olive oil
- ½ cup dry white wine
- 2 thyme sprigs
- 1 cup chicken stock, homemade (see page 260) or low-sodium store-bought
- 3 tablespoons unsalted butter, cut into pieces
- 1 tablespoon fresh lemon juice (from ½ lemon)

Preheat oven to 450°F. Rinse all chicken and pat dry with paper towels; season with salt and pepper. Heat oil in a large sauté pan over medium-high until hot but not smoking. Add chicken, skin sides down; sear until skin is browned, about 7 minutes.

Flip chicken; transfer pan to the oven. Cook until an instant-read thermometer inserted into thickest part (avoiding bone) registers 165°F, 8 to 10 minutes. Transfer chicken to a platter (cut breasts in half, if desired). Tent with parchment paper, then foil, to keep warm.

Add wine and thyme to pan; cook over medium-high, whisking, until wine has reduced slightly, about 3 minutes. Pour in stock, and cook until thickened slightly, about 3 minutes. Add butter and lemon juice; cook, whisking, until emulsified, about 1 minute. Drizzle chicken with some of the pan sauce and serve remaining sauce on the side.

Lemon-Thyme Spoonbread

A specialty of the American South, spoonbread is baked to form a thin crust on top of a soft, moist interior as it bakes. A two-quart soufflé dish has the right depth for baking (and spooning). Other baking dishes that are at least three inches deep can be used instead. Serves 4 (with leftovers)

- 4 tablespoons (½ stick) unsalted butter, plus more for dish
- 1 cup yellow cornmeal
- 2 teaspoons baking powder
- 2 teaspoons fresh thyme leaves
- 1 tablespoon finely grated lemon zest
- 1 teaspoon coarse salt
- ¼ teaspoon freshly ground pepper
- 1½ cups milk
- ½ cup heavy cream
- 3 large eggs, lightly beaten

Preheat oven to 400°F. Butter a 2-quart soufflé dish. Whisk together cornmeal, baking powder, thyme, zest, salt, and pepper. In a small saucepan, heat the milk, cream, and butter until scalding (just beginning to steam and bubble around the edges); pour over the cornmeal mixture, and whisk to combine. Whisk in the eggs until thoroughly combined.

Pour batter into prepared dish. Bake until puffy and golden on top (it will still jiggle slightly but should not be wet in the center), 20 to 25 minutes. Let cool 15 minutes before serving.

Wilted Dandelion Greens

Look for dandelion greens at farmers' markets and many supermarkets in the spring; before using, wash well to remove any grit. Slab bacon is available at deli counters or from a butcher; ask for it to be sliced about a half-inch thick (or use eight slices packaged thick-cut bacon). Serves 4

1 bunch dandelion greens (4 ounces), thick stems removed, leaves cut into large pieces (8 cups)
6 ounces slab bacon, cut into ½-inch dice
2 tablespoons plus 1 teaspoon olive oil
3 tablespoons minced shallot (1 large)
1 tablespoon Dijon mustard
3 tablespoons red wine vinegar
Coarse salt and freshly ground pepper

Place dandelion greens in a serving bowl. Cook bacon in a medium sauté pan over medium until crisp and fat has rendered, about 10 minutes. Use a slotted spoon to transfer bacon to a plate.

Pour off all but about 2 teaspoons fat from pan; add oil. Cook shallot over medium heat until softened, stirring, about 2 minutes. Add mustard and vinegar, whisking to combine; cook 30 seconds. Return bacon to pan; stir to coat. Season with salt and pepper. Pour dressing over greens; toss to coat, and serve.

Raspberries with Honey and Buttermilk

This "recipe" proves that you can serve dessert any day of the week, especially when the main ingredient is fresh fruit. Any other berries or sliced ripe stone fruits, such as peaches or nectarines, can be used in place of the raspberries. Serves 4

2 pints fresh raspberries
¼ cup honey
1 cup buttermilk

Divide raspberries evenly among four bowls. Drizzle each portion with 1 tablespoon honey, then pour ¼ cup buttermilk over berries. Serve immediately.

An easygoing meal calls for an equally modest dessert, and a bowl of raspberries fits the bill perfectly; honey adds sweetness, buttermilk lends tang (and a flavor reminiscent of Southern desserts).

A springtime supper in the garden is a delightful way to enjoy the late-day sunshine. Lemons and fresh oregano brighten baked fish, while tomatoes (a harbinger of summer) are a nice addition to saffron-flavored rice. Each plate is garnished with a handful of baby lettuces.

Spicy Stuffed Celery Sticks
Baked Flounder with Lemons and Onions
Saffron-Tomato Rice
Bread and Butter Pudding
with Strawberries

PREPARATION SCHEDULE

1. Soak bread in custard for dessert; prepare and chill celery.

2. Meanwhile, bake lemons and onions.

3. Mix cream-cheese spread.

4. Bake fish; cook rice.

5. Bake pudding and macerate strawberries while serving dinner.

Baked Flounder with Lemons and Onions

Be careful when transferring the fish from the baking dish to the plate—flounder is fragile and falls apart easily. The lemons will be tender enough to eat, rind and all. Serves 4

2   lemons, sliced into ¼-inch-thick rounds, seeds removed
2   Vidalia or sweet yellow onions, sliced into very thin rounds
4   tablespoons (½ stick) unsalted butter, cut into pieces
1   cup dry white wine
¼   cup water
1   teaspoon coarsely chopped fresh thyme leaves, plus several sprigs
    Coarse salt and freshly ground pepper
4   flounder or sole fillets (6 ounces each)

Preheat oven to 400°F. Place lemons and onions in a 9-by-13-inch glass baking dish, spreading evenly. Dot with butter; add wine and the water. Sprinkle with chopped thyme; season with salt and pepper. Bake until onions are soft and translucent, about 40 minutes.

Remove from oven. Place fish in baking dish, and season both sides with salt and pepper. Arrange several of the lemon and onion rounds over the fish, and scatter with thyme sprigs; use a spoon to baste fish with a little cooking liquid from baking dish. Bake, basting again half-way through, until fish is just opaque and cooked through, 12 to 16 minutes total (depending on thickness of fish; do not overcook).

Use a spatula to transfer fish to plates. Serve with lemons and onions, and garnish with thyme sprigs.

Saffron-Tomato Rice

Before cooking, jasmine rice should be rinsed in a sieve under cold running water until the water runs clear. This will remove some of its excess starch, for the fluffiest results. To seed the tomatoes, cut into quarters through the stem; lay quarters skin side down, and slice out flesh with a sharp knife. Serves 4

1   cup jasmine or long-grain white rice
1½ cups water
     Coarse salt and freshly ground pepper
     Pinch of saffron
2   tablespoons unsalted butter, room temperature
2   ripe beefsteak tomatoes, seeded and cut into ¼-inch dice (about 1 cup)
6   sprigs oregano, leaves picked from stem

Bring rice and the water to a boil in a medium saucepan over medium-high heat. Add a pinch of salt and the saffron; stir once to combine. Reduce heat to a simmer: Cover and cook until rice is tender and has absorbed all liquid, 16 to 18 minutes (check only during end of cooking time; the rice should be studded with holes). Remove from heat. Let steam (covered) 10 minutes, then fluff with a fork.

Transfer rice to a serving bowl. Add butter, tomatoes, and oregano leaves; toss very gently to combine. Season with salt and pepper, and serve.

Spicy Stuffed Celery Sticks

Horseradish and hot-pepper sauce add spicy heat to cream cheese in this grown-up version of stuffed celery sticks. Serves 4

- 1 bunch celery
- 8 ounces cream cheese, softened
- 2 tablespoons prepared horseradish, or to taste
- 5 drops hot-pepper sauce (such as Tabasco), or to taste
   Coarse salt and freshly ground pepper

Separate the celery stalks and rinse them free of grit; peel to remove strings, if desired. Cut the stalks into 3- to 4-inch-long pieces, leaving the tender hearts (inner stalks) whole. Wrap celery in a damp kitchen cloth or paper towels, and chill for 1 hour before serving.

In a small bowl, combine the cream cheese, horseradish, and hot-pepper sauce. Season with ½ teaspoon salt and ¼ teaspoon pepper, or to taste, and stir to combine. To serve, spread cream-cheese mixture on celery.

Bread and Butter Pudding with Strawberries

For the best results, be sure to soak bread in the custard for a full hour. Serves 4 (with leftovers)

- 4 large eggs
- ¾ cup milk
- ¾ cup heavy cream
- 2 tablespoons dark rum
- ¼ cup plus 3 tablespoons sugar
- ½ teaspoon pure vanilla extract
   Pinch of salt
- 8 thin slices day-old white sandwich bread
- 4 tablespoons (½ stick) unsalted butter, very soft
- 1 pint fresh strawberries, rinsed and hulled, cut in half

Whisk together eggs, milk, cream, rum, 3 tablespoons sugar, vanilla, and salt. Spread butter over bread. Cut slices in half to form triangles. Fit bread, buttered sides up, in a 9-inch baking dish, overlapping in a single layer. Pour egg mixture over bread; let stand at room temperature 1 hour.

Preheat oven to 400°F. Sprinkle bread with 2 tablespoons sugar. Bake until golden brown and set, about 25 minutes. Meanwhile, combine strawberries with remaining 2 tablespoons sugar. Let macerate, tossing occasionally. Serve pudding warm topped with berries (and juices).

Roses look right at home next to bread and butter pudding, a British specialty; this version includes a bit of rum for extra flavor. Macerated strawberries are sprinkled on top after baking.

summer

Summer presents a delightful conundrum: The markets are overflowing with local fruits and vegetables at their peak, yet the long, sunny days cut short any thoughts of spending hours in the kitchen. The solution? Menus that can be prepared quickly and served (or even cooked) out-doors. Now is the time to clean the grates and stock up on charcoal. Grilled burgers with a twist anchor an Independence Day worthy meal, while skewered chicken, pork kebabs, and grilled steak, fish, and pork provide ample opportunity to perfect your technique. Some menus rely on other quick-cooking methods, such as poaching, to make chicken tonnato, a variation on the classic Italian hot-weather dish, and stir-frying, for spicy shrimp served over rice noodles. Rounding out the meals are all manner of salads, including spinach and grilled corn, rice with dill and red onion, and tomato, basil, and white beans. For dessert, think fast (and fruit): a raspberry and watermelon salad is ready in min-utes, while ices, sorbets, and granitas can be quickly whisked together and then tucked into the freezer while you tend to the rest of the meal. They are light, refreshing, and just right for stretching out the evening.

summer menus

Pancetta Cheeseburgers
Balsamic Mushrooms
Tomato, Basil, and White Bean Salad
Coconut-Topped Cupcakes

PREPARATION SCHEDULE

1. Bake cupcakes, and let cool.
2. Assemble salad; let stand at least 30 minutes.
3. Meanwhile, cook pancetta; sauté mushrooms.
4. Grill burgers.
5. Frost cupcakes; sprinkle with coconut just before serving.

Pancetta Cheeseburgers

These burgers can be cooked in a grill pan or under the broiler instead of on the grill. Serves 4

- 4 thin slices pancetta (about 2 ounces)
- 1¼ pounds ground beef chuck
- ½ teaspoon chili powder
- ¼ teaspoon paprika
  Coarse salt and freshly ground pepper
- 4 ounces Italian fontina cheese, thinly sliced
- 4 hamburger buns, toasted if desired

Preheat oven to 350°F. Place pancetta on a rimmed baking sheet. Bake, flipping the slices halfway through, until crisp, about 15 minutes. Drain on paper towels.

Meanwhile, using your hands, gently mix ground beef, chili powder, paprika, ¾ teaspoon salt, and ¼ teaspoon pepper in a bowl. Gently shape into four equal-size patties (about 4 inches in diameter).

Heat grill to medium (if using a charcoal grill, coals are ready when you can hold your hand 5 inches above grill for just 5 to 6 seconds). Grill burgers 4 to 5 minutes, then flip and top with cheese. Grill to desired doneness (3 to 4 minutes more for medium-rare). Transfer to a plate, and let rest 5 minutes. To serve, top burgers with pancetta and place in buns.

{ For an out-of-the-ordinary backyard barbecue, grilled burgers are topped with slices of crisped pancetta and melted fontina cheese. They are also served with sautéed mushrooms laced with balsamic vinegar, and a summery white bean and tomato salad heady with garlic and fresh basil. A vintage tin tole tray is just right for al fresco entertaining.

Tomato, Basil, and White Bean Salad

Inspired by a very popular salad made with tomatoes, basil, and fresh mozzarella, this simple side dish features creamy cannellini beans in place of the cheese—to equally delicious effect. Serves 4

- 2 cans (19 ounces each) cannellini beans, drained and rinsed
- ½ pound small plum tomatoes, cut into 1-inch pieces
- ½ cup loosely packed fresh basil leaves, torn into ½-inch pieces
  Coarse salt and freshly ground pepper
- ¼ cup extra-virgin olive oil
- 3 small garlic cloves, minced

Combine beans, tomatoes, basil, and 1 teaspoon salt in a bowl, and season with pepper.

Heat oil in a small skillet over medium. Cook garlic, stirring constantly, until fragrant but not browned, 1½ to 2 minutes. Pour over bean mixture, and gently toss to combine. Let stand 30 minutes before serving to allow the flavors to meld. (Salad can be covered and kept at room temperature up to 4 hours.)

Balsamic Mushrooms

This side dish tastes just as good at room temperature as it does warm. Other types of mushrooms, such as cremini or baby portobello, can be used instead of white button. Serves 4

- ¼ cup olive oil
- 12 ounces white button mushrooms, halved (or quartered if large)
- 3 tablespoons balsamic vinegar
- ¼ teaspoon crushed red-pepper flakes
  Coarse salt and freshly ground black pepper

Heat oil in a medium skillet over medium-high. Add mushrooms, and cook until golden brown, stirring occasionally, about 5 minutes. Stir in vinegar, red-pepper flakes, and 1 teaspoon salt; season with black pepper. Cook 1 minute more. Transfer to a bowl, and serve.

Coconut-Topped Cupcakes

Makes 12

- ¾ cup (1½ sticks) unsalted butter, room temperature
- 1 cup granulated sugar
- 2 large eggs
- ¾ teaspoon pure vanilla extract
- 1½ cups sifted cake flour (not self-rising)
- ½ teaspoon baking powder
- ¼ teaspoon coarse salt
- ½ cup milk
- 8 ounces cream cheese, room temperature
- 1 cup confectioners' sugar
- 2 teaspoons pure coconut extract
- 2 cups sweetened flaked coconut (6 ounces)

Preheat oven to 350°F. Line a standard muffin tin with paper liners. With an electric mixer on medium-high speed, beat 1 stick butter and the granulated sugar until fluffy. Beat in eggs, one at a time, and vanilla. Reduce speed to low. Beat in flour, baking powder, and salt, then milk. Spoon into cups, filling each about three-quarters full. Bake until a cake tester inserted into centers comes out clean, about 15 minutes. Let cool on a wire rack.

With mixer on medium, beat cream cheese, remaining ½ stick butter, confectioners' sugar, and coconut extract until fluffy. Frost cupcakes; sprinkle with coconut.

These miniature cakes with cream cheese and coconut frosting end the evening with a touch of whimsy, their silver wrappers adding just the right amount of sparkle.

Broiled Black-Pepper Tofu
Soy-Lemon Dipping Sauce
Soba Noodle Salad
Baked Apricots with Almond Topping

PREPARATION SCHEDULE

1. Press tofu and prepare almond mixture for dessert.

2. Make dipping sauce; top apricots with almond mixture.

3. Cook sugar snap peas and noodles; toss together.

4. Broil tofu.

5. Bake apricots after dinner is served.

Broiled Black-Pepper Tofu

Tamari soy sauce is similar to regular soy sauce but is slightly thicker and has a richer flavor. It is available at many grocery stores. Pressing the tofu will remove excess water and allow it to soak up the peppery marinade. Refrigerate unused tofu in an airtight container, with enough cold water to cover, up to three days, changing water every day. Serves 4

- 1½ blocks firm tofu (from two 14-ounce packages)
- 2 tablespoons tamari soy sauce
- 1 tablespoon toasted sesame oil
  Freshly ground pepper
  Soy-Lemon Dipping Sauce

Cut tofu crosswise into 6 equal slices (about ¾ inch thick). Cut each slice diagonally into 2 triangles. Line a rimmed baking sheet with a double layer of paper towels. Place tofu in a single layer on top, and cover with another double layer of paper towels. Place another baking sheet on top, and weight with heavy objects (such as canned goods or a skillet); let stand 20 minutes.

Heat broiler with rack 6 inches from heat source. Stir together soy sauce, sesame oil, and ¾ teaspoon pepper in a 9-by-13-inch baking dish. Pat dry tofu with paper towels; transfer to baking dish. Turn to coat both sides with marinade. Broil, flipping once, until golden brown, about 4 minutes per side. Serve with dipping sauce.

Soy-Lemon Dipping Sauce

Besides being the perfect condiment for the tofu, this sauce makes a nice dressing for the soba noodles—just drizzle a little bit on top. Makes ½ cup

- 2 tablespoons peeled and minced fresh ginger (from a ½-inch piece)
- ¼ cup tamari soy sauce
- ½ teaspoon finely grated lemon zest
- 1 tablespoon plus 2 teaspoons fresh lemon juice
- 1 teaspoon toasted sesame oil

Whisk together ginger, soy sauce, lemon zest and juice, and sesame oil in a small bowl. Let stand at room temperature until ready to serve, up to 30 minutes. Just before serving, stir well to combine.

{ In this vegetarian meal, tofu triangles are coated in a peppery marinade and then quickly broiled until golden; a tangy sauce of soy, ginger, and lemon is served alongside for dipping. Soba noodles with carrots and sugar snap peas are healthful and satisfying. Hand-painted glasses and floral-patterned linens strike a summery mood.

Soba Noodle Salad

Made with buckwheat flour, soba noodles have a nutty flavor; look for them at Asian grocers and supermarkets. Serves 4

  Coarse salt and freshly ground pepper
 8 ounces sugar snap peas, trimmed, strings removed
12 ounces soba noodles
 1 tablespoon plus 1 teaspoon toasted sesame oil
 1 tablespoon plus 1 teaspoon peanut oil
 2 carrots (about ½ pound), shaved into thin strips using a vegetable peeler
 1 teaspoon minced peeled fresh ginger
 4 scallions, trimmed and thinly sliced crosswise
 1 tablespoon tamari soy sauce
 ¼ cup torn fresh mint, plus whole leaves for garnish

Prepare an ice-water bath. Bring a large pot of water to a boil; add salt. Blanch peas until bright green and crisp-tender, about 2 minutes. Using a slotted spoon, transfer peas to ice bath to stop the cooking; cool completely, then drain. Return water to a boil; cook noodles according to package instructions. Drain; rinse with cold water, then drain again. Transfer noodles to a large bowl. Add oils; toss to combine. Add blanched peas and remaining ingredients; season with pepper. Toss to combine. Serve at room temperature.

Baked Apricots with Almond Topping

A simple dessert features the winning combination of apricots and almonds. Other stone fruit, such as peaches or nectarines, can be substituted, but they may take longer to bake. Serves 4

1½ tablespoons unsalted butter, room temperature, plus more for baking dish
 ¼ cup whole unblanched almonds (about 1 ounce)
 3 tablespoons packed light-brown sugar
 6 apricots, halved and pitted

Preheat oven to 400°F. Butter a 9-inch baking dish or pie plate. Process almonds and brown sugar in a food processor until almonds are finely chopped. Add butter; process until just combined.

Place apricot halves, cut sides up, in prepared dish. Cover top of each apricot half generously with almond mixture, dividing evenly. Bake until apricots are soft and juicy and almond mixture is deep golden brown, 15 to 20 minutes. Transfer 3 apricot halves to each plate, and serve.

A short time in the oven softens sweet apricots and concentrates their flavor. The buttery almond-and-brown-sugar topping turns golden brown after baking, adding a pleasant crunch. Glasses of iced tea make a refreshing accompaniment.

Crisp sugar snap peas, lemony rice salad with dill, and an arugula garnish offset the richness of salmon and its accompanying creamy leek sauce. Pass the extra sauce at the table in a small bowl with a ladle. These antique seashell-patterned plates make fitting service pieces for a summer seafood dinner.

Salmon with Creamy Leeks
Dilled Rice Salad
Sugar Snap Peas with Toasted Almonds
Raspberry-Mint Gelatin Cups

PREPARATION SCHEDULE

1. Make raspberry gelatins, and chill.

2. Toast almonds for snap peas; cook rice.

3. Make leek sauce; sauté salmon.

4. Assemble rice salad, and cook peas.

5. Just before serving dessert, whip cream for gelatins.

Salmon with Creamy Leeks

Serves 4

- 3 tablespoons unsalted butter
- 3 leeks, white and pale-green parts only, sliced into ½-inch rounds (about 1½ cups) and washed well
- ⅓ cup dry white wine
- ⅓ cup heavy cream
- 2 tablespoons finely chopped fresh chives
  Coarse salt and freshly ground pepper
- ¼ cup chicken stock, homemade (see page 260) or low-sodium store-bought
- 1 tablespoon olive oil
- 4 salmon fillets (about 6 ounces each), preferably wild, skin on
- 1 bunch arugula, washed well and dried, for serving

Melt butter in a medium skillet over medium-low heat. Add leeks; simmer, stirring occasionally, 5 minutes. Add wine, and simmer until leeks are very tender, about 4 minutes. Add cream and chives; return just to a simmer. Season with salt and pepper. Remove from heat. Reserve half; transfer remaining mixture to a blender. Add stock, and puree until leek sauce is smooth.

Meanwhile, heat the oil in a large sauté pan over medium. Season salmon on both sides with salt and pepper; place skin side down in pan. Cook until well browned underneath, about 5 minutes. Flip fillets, and sauté just until fish is cooked through, about 4 minutes more; it should still be slightly pink in the center. Transfer to a platter.

Divide salmon and arugula among four plates and spoon some of the leek sauce over salmon. Garnish with reserved leek mixture and pass remaining leek sauce alongside.

Sugar Snap Peas with Toasted Almonds

Chopping half the almonds by hand results in a dish with a bit more texture. Serves 4

- ½ cup whole unblanched almonds (2½ ounces)
- 3 tablespoons unsalted butter
- 1 pound fresh sugar snap peas, trimmed, strings removed
- 3 tablespoons fresh lemon juice
  Coarse salt and freshly ground pepper

Preheat oven to 400°F. Spread almonds in a single layer on a rimmed baking sheet; toast until golden and fragrant, tossing halfway through, 8 to 10 minutes. Transfer to a plate to cool completely. Coarsely chop half the almonds on a cutting board; transfer to a small bowl. Pulse remaining half in a food processor until finely chopped, 15 to 20 times. Add to bowl with coarsely chopped almonds and stir to combine.

Melt butter in a large skillet over medium heat. Add peas, lemon juice, ½ teaspoon salt, and ¼ teaspoon pepper; cook, stirring to combine, until heated through, about 2 minutes. Sprinkle with almonds, and toss to coat.

Dilled Rice Salad

This salad is delicious warm or at room temperature; be sure to toss the rice with the dressing while still hot, when it will absorb the most flavor. Serves 4

    Coarse salt and freshly ground pepper
1   cup long-grain white rice
½   small red onion, finely chopped (about ⅓ cup)
3   tablespoons red wine vinegar
    Finely grated zest and juice of 1 lemon
2   tablespoons plus 1½ teaspoons extra-virgin olive oil
1½ teaspoons finely chopped garlic (about 2 small cloves)
3   tablespoons coarsely chopped fresh dill

Bring a medium saucepan three-quarters full of water to a boil; add 2 teaspoons salt. Stir in rice; return to a boil. Reduce heat; simmer (uncovered) until rice is tender, about 14 minutes. Drain and transfer to a bowl.

Meanwhile, mix red onion and vinegar in another bowl. Let sit 5 minutes; strain onion in a sieve, discarding vinegar. Whisk lemon juice, oil, garlic, ¾ teaspoon salt, and ¼ teaspoon pepper to combine. Drizzle lemon-juice mixture over hot rice. Add dill, lemon zest, and reserved onion; toss to combine. Serve warm or at room temperature.

Raspberry-Mint Gelatin Cups

White grape juice adds sweetness but not color to fresh-fruit gelatins. Serves 4

¾   cup water
¾   cup granulated sugar
½   bunch fresh mint, leaves picked and rinsed well (about ½ cup)
½   cup white grape juice
1   tablespoon fresh lime juice
1½ teaspoons unflavored gelatin (½ envelope)
1   container (6 ounces) fresh raspberries
½   cup heavy cream
1   tablespoon confectioners' sugar

Bring the water, granulated sugar, and mint to a boil in a medium saucepan over high heat. Reduce heat to medium; simmer 2 minutes, swirling pan to dissolve sugar. Strain syrup through a fine sieve into a bowl; discard mint.

Combine grape juice, lime juice, and gelatin in a medium heatproof bowl set over a pan of simmering water; stir until gelatin is dissolved. Remove bowl from heat; add mint syrup and berries, stirring with a wooden spoon and breaking some berries into pieces. Divide mixture among four 6-ounce bowls or ramekins. Cover with waxed paper or plastic wrap; refrigerate until firm, at least 4 hours and up to 2 days.

Just before serving, whisk the cream with an electric mixer on medium speed until soft peaks form, 3 to 4 minutes. Add confectioners' sugar, and continue beating until soft peaks return, 1 to 2 minutes. Spoon a dollop of whipped cream onto each serving.

A combination of white grape juice, lime juice, and fresh-mint simple syrup is the basis for an invigorating gelatin studded with raspberries. Dollops of lightly sweetened whipped cream echo the lovely white shade of the pedestal bowls.

Chicken marinated in a honey-and-vinegar glaze is threaded with sweet red onion wedges to make tangy kebabs, which can be baked or grilled. Raffia placemats and a handmade ceramic pitcher are as casual as the meal itself.

Cantaloupe Wedges with Feta Cheese
Honey-Glazed Chicken Skewers
Summer Squash and Olive Phyllo Tart
Espresso Cream Crunch

PREPARATION SCHEDULE

1. Marinate chicken and onion.

2. Assemble and bake tart.

3. Cook skewers.

4. Make whipped cream mixture; refrigerate.

5. Crush espresso beans and fold into cream mixture just before serving.

Honey-Glazed Chicken Skewers

You can also grill (rather than roast) the skewers: Grill over medium heat (if using a charcoal grill, coals are ready when you can hold your hand five inches above grill for just five to six seconds), brushing with marinade and turning halfway through, until the chicken is cooked through and the onions are charred, sixteen to eighteen minutes. If you use wooden skewers, soak them in water for thirty minutes before grilling to keep them from scorching. Serves 4

½ cup red wine vinegar
1 garlic clove, minced
   Coarse salt and freshly ground pepper
1 tablespoon plus 1 teaspoon honey
2 tablespoons extra-virgin olive oil
8 boneless, skinless chicken thighs (about 3 pounds), each cut into 3 pieces
1 large red onion, peeled, root end left intact, cut through the root into 8 wedges

Preheat oven to 375°F. Stir together vinegar, garlic, 1½ teaspoons salt, the honey, and oil in a large bowl; season with pepper. Add chicken and onion to the marinade. Let stand at room temperature, tossing occasionally, 15 minutes.

Thread 6 pieces of chicken and 1 onion wedge onto each of 4 skewers. Transfer threaded skewers and remaining onion wedges to a nonreactive baking sheet; drizzle marinade on top. Roast, without turning, until chicken is cooked through, 35 to 40 minutes. To serve, divide skewers and onion wedges among plates; drizzle with juices from pan.

Summer Squash and Olive Phyllo Tart

To keep phyllo dough from drying out, work with one sheet at a time and keep the rest covered with a damp kitchen towel. Unused phyllo sheets can be wrapped well in plastic and refrigerated for up to one week. Serves 4

- 3 tablespoons coarsely chopped fresh flat-leaf parsley
- 2 tablespoons coarsely chopped fresh oregano, plus sprigs for garnish (optional)
- 1 tablespoon coarsely chopped fresh thyme
- 1 garlic clove, minced
- ¼ cup extra-virgin olive oil
  Coarse salt and freshly ground pepper
- 2 small zucchini, cut into ⅛-inch-thick rounds
- 2 small yellow squash, cut into ⅛-inch-thick rounds
- 6 sheets (12 by 17 inches) frozen phyllo dough, thawed according to package instructions
- 3 tablespoons unsalted butter, melted
- ½ cup pitted Kalamata olives

Preheat oven to 375°F. Stir together chopped herbs, garlic, and 3 tablespoons oil; season with salt and pepper. Toss zucchini and squash with remaining tablespoon oil in a separate bowl; season with salt and pepper.

Unfold phyllo dough; cover sheets with a slightly damp kitchen towel. Brush a rimmed baking sheet with butter. Press 1 sheet of dough into baking sheet. Lightly brush dough with melted butter. Repeat, layering remaining 5 sheets dough and brushing each with butter.

Spread herb mixture over dough with a spoon. Arrange zucchini and squash on top, then add olives. Bake until crust is browned around edges, 25 to 30 minutes. Let cool slightly before cutting into pieces and serving; garnish with oregano sprigs, if desired.

Cantaloupe Wedges with Feta Cheese

In this summery starter, tangy feta and crushed peppercorns provide a Greek spin on the more familiar prosciutto-wrapped melon. Serves 4

- ½ teaspoon whole black peppercorns
- ½ ripe cantaloupe, seeded
- 1 block (8 ounces) feta cheese, broken into 4 pieces

Coarsely crush peppercorns with the side of a large knife (or with a mortar and pestle). Just before serving, cut cantaloupe into 4 wedges. Place 1 wedge and 1 piece of cheese on each serving plate. Sprinkle cheese with peppercorns, dividing evenly.

{ Vibrant slices of zucchini and yellow squash, plus plump Greek olives, are arranged over flaky store-bought phyllo dough for an easy side-dish tart (it would also make a nice starter).

Espresso Cream Crunch

Briefly chilling the bowl (especially if it's made of metal) keeps the cream cold and makes it easier to whip; crushing the espresso beans one at a time will prevent them from sticking together. Serve thin, crisp cookies, such as the chocolate-dipped ones shown, on the side; or offer your favorite almond wafers or biscotti. Serves 4

- 1¼   cups heavy cream
-    2   tablespoons plus 1 teaspoon sugar
-    1   teaspoon instant espresso powder (not instant coffee granules)
-    ¼   cup chocolate-covered espresso beans (about 30)

Whisk together cream, sugar, and espresso powder in a chilled bowl until soft peaks form. Refrigerate cream mixture until ready to use.

Lightly crush espresso beans on a cutting board, 1 at a time, with the side of a large knife. Just before serving, gently fold crushed espresso beans into cream mixture. Spoon into bowls.

About Instant Espresso

Instant espresso, made by first brewing espresso and then freeze-drying the liquid into quick-dissolving granules, has a deeper, more robust flavor than instant coffee, which should generally not be substituted. You can find instant espresso in either crystal or powdered form; both types are appropriate for use in baking and other desserts, although some cooks prefer to grind the crystals in a coffee mill before using. It is worth seeking out premium brands: Medaglia d'Oro (crystal) is available at many supermarkets, or you can order espresso powder from online retailers. Most recipes call for just a small amount of instant espresso; store unused powder in the freezer, either in its original packaging or another airtight container, for maximum freshness.

This fluffy whipped cream dessert packs a one-two punch of rich coffee flavor—it's laced with espresso powder and then studded with bits of crunchy chocolate-covered espresso beans.

For this Mexican meal, gorditas—crisp pan-fried corn cakes—are layered with avocado slices, shredded pork, tomato wedges, and crema, and then garnished with a sprig of cilantro. Mashed kidney beans with crumbly cotija cheese make a hearty side dish. Serve with beer, and save the tequila for dessert.

Tender Shredded Pork
Mexican Corn Cakes
Red Beans with Cheese
Tequila-Soaked Lemon Sorbet

PREPARATION SCHEDULE

1. Simmer pork; cook kidney beans.

2. Make corn-cake batter; shape into patties, and fry.

3. Broil pork.

4. Layer pork and vegetables on corn cakes.

5. Assemble dessert just before serving.

Mexican Corn Cakes

Cotija, also known as queso añejado, is a crumbly, aged white cheese; look for it in specialty food stores or Latin markets. Feta cheese can be used in its place. Serves 4

- 1½ cups *masa harina* (Mexican corn flour) or cornmeal
- ½ cup all-purpose flour
- 1 teaspoon baking powder
- ½ teaspoon coarse salt
- ½ cup grated cotija cheese
- 2 cups coarsely chopped fresh (from about 2 large ears) or frozen unthawed corn kernels
- ¾ to 1 cup warm water (110°F)
- ¼ cup safflower or other neutral-tasting oil, plus more if needed
- 1 ripe but firm avocado, halved lengthwise, pitted, peeled, and thinly sliced
  Tender Shredded Pork
- 2 ripe tomatoes, cut into thin wedges
- ½ cup Mexican *crema* or sour cream

Whisk together *masa harina*, flour, baking powder, and salt. Stir in cheese and corn. Stirring constantly, add water, ¼ cup at a time, just until mixture holds together.

Heat oil in a large cast-iron skillet over medium until hot but not smoking. Shape a heaping ⅓ cup corn mixture into a patty about ½ inch thick. Repeat, forming 8 patties total. Fry patties in two batches, turning once, until golden brown, 4 to 5 minutes per side; add more oil, if needed, between batches. Using a slotted spatula, transfer to paper towels. Tent cakes with parchment, then foil, to keep warm. Top cakes with avocado, shredded pork, 1 tablespoon *crema*, and tomato wedges. Garnish with cilantro sprigs.

Tender Shredded Pork

Reserve a few sprigs of cilantro for garnishing the corn cakes. The pork also makes a delicious filling for tacos, enchiladas, and quesadillas. Serves 4

- 1 pound pork tenderloin
- 4 cups chicken stock, homemade (see page 260) or low-sodium store-bought
- 2 small onions, finely chopped
- ½ jalapeño chile, finely chopped (ribs and seeds removed for less heat, if desired)
- ½ bunch cilantro (2½ to 3 cups loosely packed leaves; reserve a few sprigs for garnish)
- ¼ teaspoon ground cumin
- 1 dried bay leaf
  Coarse salt and freshly ground pepper
- 2 tablespoons unsalted butter, melted
- 1 tablespoon extra-virgin olive oil

Combine pork, stock, half the onions, the jalapeño, cilantro leaves, cumin, bay leaf, and ½ teaspoon salt in a medium saucepan. Bring to a boil; reduce heat to a simmer. Cook (uncovered), stirring occasionally, until an instant-read thermometer registers 138°F, 10 to 15 minutes.

Heat broiler. Remove pork from the cooking liquid, and cut meat into 2- to 3-inch-long pieces. Transfer pork to a rimmed baking sheet. Shred with two forks. Add remaining onion, and stir in butter and oil. Season with salt and pepper. Broil pork until golden brown, 5 to 7 minutes. Serve warm.

Red Beans with Cheese

Pinto beans, commonly used in Latin American cooking, would be a good substitute for kidney beans. Serves 4

- 2 cans (19 ounces each) kidney beans, drained and rinsed
- 4 cups chicken stock, homemade (see page 260) or low-sodium store-bought
- 2 dried bay leaves
- 1 onion, peeled and quartered
- 1 jalapeño chile, quartered (ribs and seeds removed for less heat, if desired)
- ½ teaspoon ground cumin
  Coarse salt
- ¼ cup grated cotija cheese

Bring beans, stock, bay leaves, onion, jalapeño, cumin, and ½ teaspoon salt to a boil in a medium saucepan. Reduce to a brisk simmer. Cook (uncovered) 15 minutes, stirring occasionally. Strain, reserving ½ cup of the cooking liquid; discard bay leaves, onion, and jalapeño.

Return beans and reserved cooking liquid to pan, and stir in 2 tablespoons cheese. Mash slightly with a potato masher until about half of the beans are broken down, leaving remaining beans whole. Season with salt. Serve warm, sprinkled with remaining 2 tablespoons cheese.

Tequila-Soaked Lemon Sorbet

Look for a premium tequila, preferably reposado, which is aged less than a year; añejo (aged more than a year) would be too strong for this recipe. Serves 4

- 1 pint lemon sorbet
- ¼ cup best-quality tequila
  Finely grated zest of 2 limes

Using an ice-cream scoop, place 2 scoops of sorbet into each of four glasses. Drizzle 1 tablespoon tequila over sorbet in each glass, and then sprinkle with lime zest. Serve immediately.

This ultra-quick dessert is reminiscent of a frozen margarita—doubly so when served in tumblers instead of bowls. Lemon sorbet is spiked with a splash of tequila, then sprinkled with finely grated lime zest.

Spicy Stir-Fried Shrimp
Rice Noodles with Coconut Milk
Braised Bok Choy
Sorbet with Wonton Crisps

PREPARATION SCHEDULE

1. Bake wonton wrappers.
2. Boil noodles; make coconut sauce.
3. Braise bok choy.
4. Cook shrimp.
5. Assemble dessert just before serving.

Rice Noodles with Coconut Milk

This dish — similar to a noodle soup, with a vibrant broth—is also delicious by itself, without the shrimp. Thin rice noodles, called rice vermicelli, turn a lovely shade of white once cooked; look for them at Asian grocers and supermarkets. When cooking with lemongrass, trim off the grassy end and use only the bulbous stalks, crushing them lightly with the side of a large knife, just to release their flavor. Serves 4

Coarse salt
8 ounces rice vermicelli (or angel hair pasta)
1 can (14 ounces) unsweetened coconut milk
1¾ cups chicken stock, homemade (see page 260) or low-sodium store-bought
1 cup loosely packed cilantro leaves, plus more for garnish
½ cup loosely packed basil, plus more for garnish
4 garlic cloves, halved
1 piece (about 2 inches) fresh ginger, peeled and cut into ⅛-inch-thick rounds
2 small fresh red chiles, halved lengthwise, stems removed
2 tablespoons Asian fish sauce (such as *nam pla*)
1 fresh lemongrass stalk, bottom 4 inches only, crushed lightly with the side of a long knife
1 tablespoon sugar
1 to 2 tablespoons fresh lime juice
Spicy Stir-Fried Shrimp (recipe follows)

Bring a large pot of water to a boil; add salt. Cook rice noodles until al dente, about 2 minutes. Drain; rinse with cold water, and drain again.

Bring coconut milk and stock to a gentle simmer in a medium saucepan over medium-low heat. Process cilantro, basil, garlic, ginger, and 1 chile in a food processor until coarsely chopped, about 5 seconds; add to stock mixture along with fish sauce (if using), lemongrass, and sugar. Simmer about 5 minutes to allow flavors to infuse; discard lemongrass.

Add noodles; cook until just heated through, about 1 minute. Remove from heat. Stir in lime juice. Finely chop remaining chile. To serve, divide noodles and broth among four bowls; top with cilantro, basil, chopped chile, and shrimp.

{ This easy-to-prepare pan-Asian meal requires little cooking to coax out the flavors of the food. Shrimp and baby bok choy are seasoned with chiles and soy sauce; ginger, lemongrass, and fresh herbs flavor the broth for quick-cooking rice. Green porcelain bowls brilliantly set off the bright herb garnishes.

Spicy Stir-Fried Shrimp

This dish gets its fiery heat from Asian chili sauce, which, unlike American chili sauce, is very thick, like a paste, and perfect for using both in cooking and as a table condiment. The shrimp are equally good served with cooked rice. Serves 4

    1   tablespoon safflower or other neutral-tasting oil
    1   shallot, thinly sliced
    1   pound large shrimp (16 count), peeled and deveined (see page 260), tails left intact
    2   tablespoons Asian chili sauce
    1   tablespoon sugar
        Coarse salt and freshly ground pepper

Heat oil in a large skillet over medium-high until hot but not smoking. Cook shallot, stirring occasionally, until softened and light golden, 2 to 3 minutes.

Add shrimp, chili sauce, and sugar; cook, stirring constantly, until shrimp are pink and opaque throughout, 3 to 4 minutes. Season with salt and pepper, and serve immediately.

Braised Bok Choy

Baby bok choy, which is more tender than the full-size version, is sold at Asian markets and many grocery stores. If you can't find baby bok choy, use one head of regular bok choy. Before cooking, cut it in half lengthwise, and cut each half into quarters. Serves 4

    1   tablespoon safflower or other neutral-tasting oil
    8   heads baby bok choy, trimmed, halved lengthwise if large
    ¼   cup chicken stock, homemade (see page 260) or low-sodium store-bought, or water
    3   tablespoons soy sauce

Heat oil in a large skillet over medium-high until hot but not smoking. Add bok choy in a single layer; cook, turning once, until just golden, about 2 minutes. Add stock and soy sauce. Reduce heat to medium; cover, and simmer until bok choy is tender, about 5 minutes. Use tongs or a slotted spoon to transfer bok choy to a serving platter.

Cook liquid in skillet over medium-high heat until reduced by half, 1 to 2 minutes. Pour over bok choy.

Buying and Preparing Shrimp

As with all seafood, shrimp are best purchased (and cooked) when just caught. If you don't have access to a fresh supply, look for shrimp labeled "flash-frozen" (frozen at sea), which can be purchased in advance and thawed when needed. If you choose to use fresh shrimp from a fishmonger, buy it on the day you plan to use it. Only select shrimp that smell fresh, like salt air (never fishy). Peel the shrimp (leaving the tail intact, as desired), then devein them by making a shallow incision down the middle of the back with a sharp knife (no special tool required) and scraping or pulling out the dark vein.

Cooking vegetables whole, such as the baby bok choy shown here, not only helps preserve their nutrients, but also makes a lovely presentation.

Sorbet with Wonton Crisps

Other sorbet flavors, such as passion fruit and coconut, are also good options. Serves 4

- 8 square or round wonton wrappers (thawed if frozen)
- 1½ teaspoons sugar
- ½ teaspoon ground ginger
   Pinch of salt
- 1 large egg yolk
- 1 tablespoon heavy cream
- 4 teaspoons white or black sesame seeds, or a mixture
- 1 pint mango sorbet, for serving

Preheat oven to 350°F. Arrange wonton wrappers in a single layer on a parchment-lined baking sheet.

Stir together sugar, ginger, and salt. Whisk together egg yolk and cream in another bowl for egg wash. Brush wontons with egg wash, and sprinkle each with about ½ teaspoon sesame seeds and a scant ¼ teaspoon sugar mixture. Bake until wontons are golden and crisp, 8 to 10 minutes. Let cool completely on sheet on a wire rack. Serve with sorbet.

About Wonton Wrappers

Wonton wrappers, also called "wonton skins," are very versatile. The fresh sheets of pasta can be stuffed and steamed, boiled, fried, or baked. Although they're traditionally formed into dumplings, the wrappers can also be used in place of fresh Italian pasta dough to make easy ravioli or tortellini. Or, you can bake or fry them to make savory or sweet crisps to serve with hors d'oeuvres or dessert. Look for the wrappers at Asian food stores and most supermarkets, either in the freezer section or next to tofu in the produce aisle. They're usually sold in small rectangular, square, or round sheets, which are stacked and wrapped in plastic. Work with one wrapper at a time, and cover the rest with damp kitchen or paper towel to keep them moist, as they dry out easily. Freeze unused wrappers, tightly wrapped, up to two months.

Sugared wonton wrappers flecked with two types of sesame seeds are baked to a delightful crisp, then served with mango sorbet for a tropical taste befitting the rest of the meal.

A relaxed backyard dinner, cooked mostly on the grill, showcases a bounty of late-summer produce, including new potatoes, baby spinach, and corn cut from the cob. A blender makes easy work of a zesty cold soup that relies on a surplus of tomatoes at their peak, while the gelatin dessert features just-picked blackberries. Red-and-white tea towels and paisley napkins combine to create charming place settings.

Blender Gazpacho
Grilled Steak with Blue Cheese Potatoes
Spinach and Grilled-Corn Salad
Blackberry–Red Wine Gelatin

PREPARATION SCHEDULE

1. Make gelatin, and chill to set.

2. Blend and refrigerate gazpacho; heat grill.

3. Marinate steak; boil potatoes.

4. Grill corn; make salad dressing.

5. Grill steak, then potatoes; toss salad.

Grilled Steak with Blue Cheese Potatoes

In this meat-and-potatoes dish, everything is grilled at the same time; the steak is first marinated for added flavor, and the potatoes are boiled so they will be fluffy and tender inside their crisp grilled exteriors. Blue cheese is a classic steakhouse offering; place it on the potatoes as soon as they come off the grill, so the cheese will begin to melt. Serves 4

- 3 garlic cloves, coarsely chopped
- 3 tablespoons coarsely chopped fresh rosemary, plus sprigs for garnish
- ¼ cup plus 2 tablespoons Worcestershire sauce
- 2 tablespoons extra-virgin olive oil, plus more for brushing potatoes
- Coarse salt and freshly ground pepper
- 1¾ pounds skirt steak, cut into 6-inch-long pieces
- 1½ pounds red new potatoes
- 3 ounces blue cheese, crumbled

Heat grill to high (if using a charcoal grill, coals are ready when you can hold your hand 5 inches above grill for just 2 seconds). Stir together garlic, rosemary, Worcestershire sauce, and oil in a nonreactive dish; season with pepper. Place steak in dish; turn to coat evenly with marinade. Marinate 15 minutes at room temperature, turning once (or up to overnight in the refrigerator, covered tightly).

Cover potatoes in a medium saucepan with cold water; add a pinch of salt. Bring to a boil. Reduce heat; simmer until just tender when pierced with a knife, about 15 minutes. Drain; let cool slightly. Slice potatoes in half. Brush cut sides with some oil; season with salt and pepper.

Grill steak, turning once, 3 to 4 minutes per side for medium-rare. Transfer to a platter to rest. Meanwhile, grill potatoes, turning once, until golden, about 5 minutes. Sprinkle with cheese.

Thinly slice steak against the grain. Serve with potatoes; garnish with rosemary sprigs.

A pureed gazpacho begins the meal on a refreshing note; thin cucumber rounds make a crisp garnish.

Blender Gazpacho

True gazpacho relies on bread for body. Day-old bread is just dry enough to provide a bit of texture once pureed, or you can dry out fresh bread: Remove the crusts, cut or tear bread into small pieces, then spread on a rimmed baking sheet and leave out at room temperature overnight, or place in a 250-degree oven for about thirty minutes. Serves 4

- 1 cup small pieces white bread (torn from 3 slices day-old rustic bread, crusts removed)
- 1 small garlic clove, minced
- 2 tablespoons red wine vinegar
- ¾ cup cold water
- ½ English cucumber, cut into 1-inch pieces, plus 8 very thin slices, for garnish
- 1½ cups coarsely chopped roasted red bell peppers
- 2 pounds beefsteak tomatoes, cut into quarters
- 2 tablespoons extra-virgin olive oil
  Coarse salt and freshly ground pepper

Stir together bread, garlic, vinegar, and the water in a bowl. Transfer mixture to a blender along with the chopped cucumber and roasted peppers; process until smooth. Transfer to a large bowl.

Puree half of the tomatoes in the blender, and transfer to the bowl with cucumber mixture. Puree remaining tomatoes, slowly adding oil while blender is running. Transfer mixture to the bowl; whisk to combine. Stir in 1½ teaspoons salt; season with pepper. Refrigerate, covered, until chilled, at least 30 minutes (or up to overnight).

To serve, divide gazpacho among four bowls. Garnish each with 2 cucumber rounds.

Spinach and Grilled-Corn Salad

Grilled corn kernels cut from the cob add smoky flavor to a simple, tossed salad of baby spinach and red onion. Serves 4

- 2 ears corn, shucked
- 3 tablespoons extra-virgin olive oil, plus more for brushing
  Coarse salt and freshly ground pepper
- 1 tablespoon balsamic vinegar
- 6 ounces baby spinach
- ½ red onion, thinly sliced into half-moons

Lightly brush corn with oil, then season with salt and pepper. Grill corn over high heat (see page 105), turning, until tender and blackened in places, about 8 minutes. Let cool slightly. Standing ears on one end, use a sharp knife to carefully cut off kernels.

Put vinegar in a small bowl; add oil in a slow, steady stream, whisking until emulsified. Combine spinach, onion, and grilled corn in a serving bowl; season with salt and pepper. Toss salad with dressing just before serving.

Using Powdered Gelatin

Gelatin is a versatile thickener that is primarily used for desserts, and not only the popular instant mixes. Most home cooks rely on the powdered form, sold in boxes of ¼-ounce packets (each scant tablespoon), although professional bakers often prefer to use gelatin in sheets (which do not impart any graininess). To activate, the powder should first be allowed to "soften" (or moisten and separate) in cold liquid (usually water or fruit juice) for about five minutes before dissolving in hot (not boiling) liquid, such as the wine used here. Cooling the mixture in an ice-water bath will help the gelatin mixture set more quickly. Whole or chopped fruit is a flavorful and visually appealing addition. Never use fresh or frozen pineapple (canned is fine), figs, kiwi fruit, guava, or papaya, all of which contain an enzyme that breaks down gelatin and causes it to lose its thickening properties.

Blackberry–Red Wine Gelatin

You can use a glass or ceramic dish instead of a metal one, but the gelatin will take longer to set. To unmold, place a small cutting board on top of the dish and flip over, holding onto both tightly; then wiggle dish and tap to release gelatin. Serves 4

- ½ cup unsweetened apple juice
- ½ cup water
- 1 tablespoon plus 1 teaspoon unflavored gelatin
- 1 cup full-bodied red wine, such as zinfandel or syrah
- ¼ cup plus 1 tablespoon sugar
- 1 pint fresh blackberries, plus more berries for garnish
  Fresh mint leaves, for garnish

Prepare an ice-water bath. Combine juice and water in a bowl; sprinkle with gelatin. Let soften 5 minutes. In a saucepan, bring wine and sugar to a boil, stirring to dissolve sugar. Add berries. Reduce heat; simmer 5 minutes. Slowly stir wine mixture into gelatin mixture. Transfer bowl to ice bath; stir gently until cool, 5 minutes.

Pour mixture into a 9-by-5-by-2½-inch nonreactive metal loaf pan. Refrigerate, covered, until set, about 1½ hours. To unmold, set bottom of pan in warm water until gelatin loosens, about 2 seconds; invert onto a cutting board. Use a knife to break seal along edges if necessary. To serve, use a large spoon to scoop gelatin onto plates. Garnish with a few blackberries and mint leaves.

Juicy blackberries lend sweet-tart flavor and intense color to this grown-up gelatin; a jammy red wine, such as zinfandel, spices up its fruity taste and adds depth. A slab of white marble makes a lovely serving platter—and helps keep the gelatin cool.

Grilled Striped Bass
Corn and Clam Chowder Sauce
Oyster Biscuits
Watermelon-Raspberry Salad

PREPARATION SCHEDULE

1. Assemble fruit salad; let macerate.

2. Marinate fish fillets.

3. Bake oyster biscuits.

4. Make chowder sauce.

5. Grill fish.

Grilled Striped Bass

Striped bass can be replaced with other firm, white-fleshed fish, such as black sea bass, halibut, or even trout. Be sure to marinate the fish no longer than thirty minutes, or the citrus juice can start to "cook" the flesh. The fillets can be served on their own, hot or at room temperature. Serves 4

¼ cup extra-virgin olive oil

3 tablespoons fresh lemon juice (from 1 to 2 lemons)

3 or 4 sprigs thyme or oregano

2 garlic cloves, smashed
   Coarse salt and freshly ground pepper

4 fillets striped bass, skin on (about 6 ounces each)
   Fresh chives, cut into ¼-inch lengths, for garnish (optional)
   Lemon wedges, for garnish (optional)

Combine oil, lemon juice, thyme, garlic, and ⅛ teaspoon pepper in a large shallow nonreactive bowl. Add fish to marinade, and turn to coat; cover with plastic wrap, and place in the refrigerator 30 minutes.

Meanwhile, heat grill to medium-high (if using a charcoal grill, coals are ready when you can hold your hand 5 inches above grill for just 3 to 4 seconds). Remove fish from marinade, letting excess drip off. Place on grill, skin side down, and season with salt. Grill until skin is lightly browned and starting to crisp, 1 to 2 minutes. Carefully turn fillets, and cook until well browned and cooked through (center will be opaque), 5 to 6 minutes. Garnish with chives and lemon wedges, if desired. To serve, divide chowder sauce among shallow bowls; top each with a fillet. Arrange clams around fish.

{ Inspired by the cuisine of the New England shoreline, this meal calls for fish fillets grilled and served on top of creamy chowder sauce made with clams and corn; miniature biscuits stand in for traditional oyster crackers. The brothy base demands a spoon, which can also be used to break apart the flaky fish for incorporating into the dish, one spoonful at a time.

Corn and Clam Chowder Sauce

This sauce is intended to be brothy, not thick like a true chowder, since it will be topped with the grilled fish for more substance. When cutting the corn kernels from the cobs, stand the ears in a wide shallow bowl to catch all the scrapings and run the dull side of the knife back over the scraped cob to extract the "milk." Serves 4

- ½ cup dry white wine
- 4 dozen Manila or littleneck clams or cockles (about 2 pounds), cleaned (see page 260)
- 1 tablespoon unsalted butter
- 2 shallots, thinly sliced
- 1 celery stalk, thinly sliced
- 2 Yukon Gold or russet potatoes, cut into ¾-inch pieces
- 2 cups fresh corn kernels (from about 3 ears), plus scrapings from cobs
- 1 sprig thyme
- 1 dried bay leaf
- 1 cup heavy cream
  Freshly ground pepper

Pour wine into a large, wide saucepan; bring to a simmer over medium-high heat. Add clams; cover tightly, and cook over medium heat until clams open, 6 to 8 minutes. Using a slotted spoon, transfer clams to a bowl (discard any that don't open). Strain liquid through a cheesecloth-lined sieve into a large liquid measuring cup or small bowl, leaving grit and sand behind.

Rinse saucepan, and melt butter over medium heat. Add shallots and celery; cook, stirring frequently, until they begin to soften, about 4 minutes. Add potatoes, along with corn kernels and scrapings, thyme, and bay leaf. Add strained cooking liquid and the cream, and stir to combine. Cover; bring to a rapid simmer. Reduce heat to medium-low, and simmer gently until potatoes are tender, 20 to 25 minutes.

Arrange clams on top; cover, and continue cooking just until heated through, about 5 minutes. Remove from heat; season with pepper, and serve immediately.

Oyster Biscuits

You can make the biscuits up to one week ahead; store in an airtight container at room temperature. Makes about 2 dozen

- 1 cup all-purpose flour, plus more for dusting
- ¾ teaspoon coarse salt, plus more for sprinkling
- 1 teaspoon baking powder
- ½ teaspoon ground cumin or coriander
  Pinch of cayenne pepper
- 2 tablespoons unsalted butter, cold
- ⅓ cup milk

Preheat oven to 350°F. In a food processor, pulse to combine flour, salt, baking powder, cumin, and cayenne. Add butter; pulse until coarse crumbs form. With machine running, slowly add milk through the feed tube, just until dough comes together.

Turn out dough onto a lightly floured surface, and knead one or two times, until smooth. Roll out to ¼ inch thick. Sprinkle with salt, and roll lightly to make it adhere. Using a 1½-inch round cookie cutter, cut out dough, and transfer shapes to an ungreased baking sheet. Gather together scraps, and reroll to cut out additional biscuits, if desired. Bake until lightly golden, and interior is flaky, 20 to 22 minutes. Transfer pan to a wire rack to cool slightly before serving.

Watermelon-Raspberry Salad

The salad can be served chilled or at room temperature. Serves 4

- 1 piece (4½ pounds) watermelon, peeled, seeded, and cut into 1-inch cubes (about 4 cups)
- 1 pint fresh raspberries
  Juice of 1 lemon
- ¼ cup sugar
  Vanilla ice cream, for serving (optional)

Place watermelon in a large bowl, and add raspberries, lemon juice, and sugar; toss to combine. Let stand (at room temperature or in the refrigerator) 30 to 45 minutes, tossing occasionally. Serve with vanilla ice cream, if desired.

{ Watermelon and raspberries combine in a summer fruit salad that is delicious on its own or over scoops of ice cream. It is the perfect ending to a rich meal.

Turkey burgers are a satisfying alternative to those made with beef, and you don't even need to heat up the grill to cook them. With chopped tomato salad and creamy corn on the side, plus blackberry-shortbread squares for dessert, the meal is a flavorful ode to summer.

Herbed Turkey Burgers
Mixed Tomato Salad
Creamed Corn
Blackberry Shortbread Squares

PREPARATION SCHEDULE

1. Assemble and bake dessert.
2. Form turkey patties.
3. Cook creamed corn.
4. Meanwhile, make tomato salad.
5. Sauté burgers.

Herbed Turkey Burgers

If you prefer, you can cook the burgers on a medium-high grill, flipping once, for about four minutes per side. Serves 4

- 2 tablespoons olive oil
- 2 shallots, minced
- 1 pound ground turkey, preferably 7% fat
- ¼ cup loosely packed fresh mint leaves, finely chopped
- ¼ cup loosely packed fresh flat-leaf parsley leaves, finely chopped
- 2 teaspoons Dijon mustard, plus more for serving
  Coarse salt and freshly ground pepper
- 4 rustic rolls, for serving
  Boston lettuce, for serving

Heat 1 tablespoon oil in a medium sauté pan over medium. Cook shallots, stirring, until soft and translucent, about 2 minutes. Remove from heat; let cool slightly.

In a large bowl, gently but thoroughly mix turkey, shallots, mint, parsley, and mustard. Season with 1 teaspoon salt and ¼ teaspoon pepper. Gently form mixture into four equal-size patties (about 4 inches in diameter).

Heat remaining tablespoon oil in a large sauté pan over medium. Add patties, and cook until brown underneath, about 4 minutes. Turn, and continue cooking until other side is brown and center is no longer pink, about 4 minutes more. Transfer to plates; serve immediately with rolls, lettuce, and mustard.

Creamed Corn

This side dish makes good use of fresh corn at its peak, and is a nice alternative to corn on the cob. Serves 4

- 2 tablespoons olive oil
- 1 jalapeño chile (ribs and seeds removed for less heat, if desired), diced
- 8 ears corn, kernels cut from cobs
- ¼ cup heavy cream
- 1¼ cups milk
  Coarse salt and freshly ground pepper

Heat oil in a large sauté pan over medium-high. Add jalapeño, and cook 1 minute. Add corn; cook, stirring, until kernels are tender but not browned, about 5 to 7 minutes. Remove from heat.

Transfer 1½ cups cooked corn to a food processor; add cream and milk. Process until mixture is very smooth, about 3 minutes. Strain through a fine sieve into a medium bowl, pressing down on the solids with a flexible spatula to extract as much liquid as possible (about 1½ cups).

Return strained liquid to sauté pan, and stir to combine with remaining corn mixture. Cook over medium-high heat, stirring frequently, until reduced and thickened, 10 to 12 minutes. Remove from heat, and season with salt and pepper. Serve hot.

Mixed Tomato Salad

A combination of beefsteak and red, yellow, and orange cherry tomatoes produces the most colorful presentation, but any ripe tomatoes will work. The salad can be spooned over the burgers, or served on the side. It would also work well with grilled fish or chicken. Serves 4

- ¼ pound beefsteak tomatoes
- ¾ pound cherry tomatoes
- 2 tablespoons extra-virgin olive oil
- 2 garlic cloves, thinly sliced
- 4 sprigs oregano, leaves picked from stems
   Coarse salt and freshly ground pepper
- 1 tablespoon balsamic vinegar
- ½ cup black olives, pitted and cut into small pieces

Core beefsteak tomatoes; cut into bite-size chunks. Halve cherry tomatoes. Combine in a serving dish.

Heat oil in a small skillet over medium. Add garlic, and cook just until it is golden brown, about 2 minutes. Remove from heat; let cool slightly, and add oregano.

Season tomatoes with 1 teaspoon salt and ¼ teaspoon pepper. Pour warm garlic mixture, including oil, over the top. Add vinegar and olives; toss well to combine.

Blackberry Shortbread Squares

Leftover squares can be stored up to three days at room temperature in an airtight container. Dust with confectioners' sugar before serving. Makes 12

- ¾ cup (1½ sticks) unsalted butter, room temperature, plus more for pan
- 1¾ cups all-purpose flour, plus more for dusting
- ⅔ cup whole blanched almonds (about 3½ ounces)
- ½ teaspoon salt
- ½ teaspoon ground cinnamon
- ¾ cup plus 2 tablespoons confectioners' sugar, plus more for dusting
- ¼ teaspoon pure almond extract
- 2 pints blackberries (about 4 cups)

Preheat oven to 350°F. Butter a 9-by-13-inch baking pan. Line with parchment paper; butter parchment, and dust with flour, tapping out excess. Arrange almonds in a single layer on a rimmed baking sheet. Toast, tossing occasionally, until dark golden, 12 to 15 minutes; transfer to a plate to cool completely.

Pulse almonds in a food processor until finely ground. Whisk together flour, ground almonds, salt, and cinnamon in a bowl.

With an electric mixer on medium-high speed, beat butter and ¾ cup plus 1 tablespoon confectioners' sugar until pale and fluffy, about 3 minutes. Mix in almond extract. Add flour mixture in two batches, mixing just until a crumbly dough forms.

Press all but 1 cup dough into bottom of prepared pan. Scatter berries evenly over dough. Sprinkle with remaining tablespoon sugar; crumble reserved dough evenly on top. Bake, rotating pan halfway through, until crust is golden, 40 to 45 minutes. Let cool completely on a wire rack. To serve, cut into 12 squares; dust with confectioners' sugar.

Almond-flavored shortbread is used for both a quick press-in-the-pan crust and a crumbly topping in these blackberry squares. Feel free to substitute other seasonal berries—blueberries, raspberries, or chopped strawberries—or chopped cherries or other stone fruits.

Avocado and Lemon on Toasted Rustic Bread
Seared Tuna in Tomato-Basil Sauce
Green Beans with Lemon Butter
Peaches in Honey Syrup

PREPARATION SCHEDULE

1. Blanch peaches and make syrup; toast bread.
2. Sear tuna; make tomato-basil sauce.
3. Meanwhile, blanch green beans; toss with lemon butter.
4. Prepare avocado mixture, and serve.
5. Assemble dessert just before serving.

Seared Tuna in Tomato-Basil Sauce

Serves 4

- ¼ cup plus 2 tablespoons olive oil
- 1½ pounds ahi or yellowfin tuna (1 inch thick), cut into 1-inch chunks
- Coarse salt and freshly ground pepper
- 1 yellow onion, finely chopped (about 1 cup)
- 2 cups (about 12 ounces) cherry tomatoes, halved
- ½ cup dry white wine or water
- ¼ cup coarsely chopped fresh basil

In a large skillet, heat 2 tablespoons oil over medium-high until hot but not smoking. Season tuna generously with salt and pepper. Arrange half the tuna in skillet in a single layer. Cook until golden brown but still slightly pink inside, turning once, about 3 minutes. Transfer to a platter; tent with parchment paper, then foil, to keep warm. Add another 2 tablespoons oil; repeat to cook remaining tuna.

Wipe skillet with paper towels. Add remaining 2 tablespoons oil. Cook onion over medium heat, stirring occasionally, until golden brown and soft, 6 to 8 minutes. Add tomatoes and wine; simmer, stirring often, until the tomatoes' skins just begin to shrivel, 3 to 5 minutes. Reduce heat until mixture barely simmers and cook until sauce thickens slightly, about 5 minutes more.

Add basil, and cook, stirring, just until wilted. Season with salt and pepper. To serve, divide tuna among four plates, and spoon warm sauce over and around tuna.

Green Beans with Lemon Butter

You can replace green beans with haricots verts or wax beans in this recipe, depending on what's available. Serves 4

- Coarse salt and freshly ground pepper
- 1 pound green beans, stem ends trimmed
- 2 tablespoons unsalted butter, cut into small pieces
- 1 tablespoon finely grated lemon zest

Fill a 4-quart saucepan three-quarters full with water. Bring to a boil over high heat, and add 1 tablespoon salt. Blanch the green beans until crisp-tender, 4 to 5 minutes. Drain, and immediately return beans to saucepan.

Add butter and zest, and toss to combine. Season with salt and pepper; serve warm.

{ This menu is at once simple and sophisticated. Seared tuna is served with a tomato-basil sauce prepared in the same pan; blanched green beans are tossed with a bit of butter and lemon zest. Lemon also flavors the avocado side dish, which is spread on top of toasted bread. Serve more bread on the side, with Niçoise or other olives for nibbling.

Avocado and Lemon on Toasted Rustic Bread

Choose a ripe avocado that gives slightly when gently pressed. Use a richly flavored extra-virgin olive oil, and good-quality sea salt, such as fleur de sel or Maldon. Serves 4

 2 ripe avocados
 1 to 2 tablespoons extra-virgin olive oil, or to taste
 2 tablespoons fresh lemon juice
    Coarse sea salt and freshly ground pepper
    Toasted rustic bread, for serving

Halve avocados lengthwise. Twist halves to separate them, and remove pits with a sharp, heavy knife. Run a large spoon between the flesh and skin, scooping out the flesh in one piece; discard skins. Slice avocados into wedges, and place on a serving platter. Drizzle with oil and lemon juice, and season with salt and pepper; mash slightly with a fork. Serve immediately with toasted bread, spreading avocado mixture on top.

Peaches in Honey Syrup

The peaches should be ripe but not too soft, so they will retain their shape when blanched and peeled. Adding the skins to the honey syrup lends flavor and rosy color. Use a good-quality honey for the most flavorful sauce. Serves 4

 4 ripe but firm medium peaches
 ½ cup honey, such as wildflower

Using a sharp knife, lightly score an X in the bottom (not stem end) of each peach.

Prepare a large ice-water bath. Fill a 4-quart saucepan with enough cold water to cover peaches; remove peaches, and bring water to a boil over high heat. Return peaches to pot, and blanch until skins just begin to pull away from fruit, about 1 minute. Using a spoon, transfer peaches to ice bath to stop the cooking; cool completely. Remove skins, reserving peaches and skins. Cover peaches with plastic wrap.

Pour off all but 2 cups of cooking liquid in pan; add skins and honey. Bring to a boil; reduce heat and cook at a rapid simmer until reduced to 1 cup, about 20 minutes. Strain liquid through a fine sieve set over a bowl, and discard skins; let cool. To serve, place a whole peach in each of four bowls, and spoon syrup over peaches.

Choosing a Ripe Peach

A peach's scarlet blush has more to do with variety than ripeness. When choosing peaches, look instead at the background color, which should be yellow or cream; avoid fruits with a green tint, as they are underripe and will not continue to sweeten. A ripe peach will also have fragrant flesh that is slightly soft, but you can soften a too-firm peach: enclose it in a paper bag—which concentrates ethylene gas, a natural ripening agent—and let it stand on the kitchen counter for two or three days. Ripe peaches should be eaten right away, but can be refrigerated two to four days.

A juicy peach is made even more delectable by blanching first to remove the peel, then drizzling generously with honey syrup. For an indulgent touch, serve with a bar of bittersweet chocolate.

Pounded to a delicate thinness, pork paillards cook in just two minutes on the grill. In this menu they are paired with a pasta dish brimming with seasonal green vegetables and topped with a mustard vinaigrette. Choose a lean white wine, such as pinot gris or grüner veltliner; a dry Alsatian riesling would also be appropriate. Here, the wine is served in cordial glasses; bone-handled flatware and red fringed linen napkins complete the place settings.

Mushroom and Goat Cheese Crostini
Grilled Pork Paillards
Pasta Verde
Cherry Ice

PREPARATION SCHEDULE

1. Combine cherry mixture; freeze (stir after 20 minutes, then scrape every 10 minutes).
2. Pound pork chops and marinate; toast bread for crostini.
3. Boil pasta, and cook vegetables; toss together with vinaigrette.
4. Sauté mushrooms; assemble crostini, and serve.
5. Grill pork.

Grilled Pork Paillards

Paillards are simply pork chops (or chicken cutlets) that have been pounded to a uniform thickness for even cooking; because they are so thin, the pieces cook very quickly. The pork can also be cooked on a grill pan; heat the pan over medium-high for five minutes before adding paillards. Serves 4

- 4 boneless pork chops (each 6 ounces and ¾ inch thick)
- ¼ cup balsamic vinegar
- ¼ cup extra-virgin olive oil
  Coarse salt and freshly ground pepper
  Fresh basil, for garnish
  Halved or quartered cherry tomatoes, for garnish

Heat grill to medium-high (if using a charcoal grill, coals are ready when you can hold your hand 5 inches above grill for just 3 to 4 seconds). Place pork chops between two layers of plastic wrap on a work surface. Using a meat pounder, pound to a ¼-inch thickness. Transfer to a large resealable plastic bag or nonreactive container. Add balsamic vinegar and oil. Refrigerate, covered, 15 minutes.

Remove pork from marinade (discard marinade); pat dry with paper towels and season both sides with salt and pepper. Grill pork until cooked through and browned on both sides, about 1 minute per side. Serve hot, garnished with basil and tomatoes.

Pasta Verde

Serves 4

- 1 tablespoon coarse-grain mustard
- 2 tablespoons white wine or sherry vinegar
- ¼ cup extra-virgin olive oil
  Coarse salt and freshly ground pepper
- 1 pound gemelli or other short pasta shape
- 1 sweet onion, halved lengthwise, then cut crosswise ¼ inch thick
- 2 small zucchini, halved lengthwise, then cut crosswise ¼ inch thick
- 8 ounces snap peas, trimmed, tough strings removed
- 3 ounces baby spinach (or 1 bunch regular spinach, tough stems removed and leaves coarsely chopped)
- 1 small bunch scallions, trimmed and thinly sliced
- ¼ cup loosely packed fresh basil leaves, thinly sliced

Bring a large pot of water to a boil. Whisk together mustard and vinegar; slowly add 2 tablespoons oil, whisking constantly until emulsified. Season with salt and pepper.

Once water is boiling, add 2 tablespoons salt. Cook pasta until al dente according to package instructions. Drain; return to pot.

Meanwhile, heat remaining 2 tablespoons oil in a large skillet over medium. Cook onion until just softened, stirring occasionally, about 4 minutes. Add zucchini; cook, stirring, until tender, 2 to 3 minutes. Add snap peas; cook, stirring, until crisp-tender, about 2 minutes.

Remove pan from heat; stir in spinach, scallions, and basil. Add to pasta along with vinaigrette; toss well to combine. Serve warm or at room temperature.

Mushroom and Goat Cheese Crostini

Look for chanterelle mushrooms at specialty food shops or farmers' markets; shiitake, oyster, or any combination of other mushrooms can be used instead. To clean chanterelles, gently scrub with a vegetable brush (or wipe with a paper towel); do not rinse. Cut the goat cheese into rounds while still chilled, then let them come to room temperature. Serves 4

- 2 tablespoons extra-virgin olive oil, plus more for brushing
- 1 shallot, thinly sliced into rings
- 8 ounces chanterelles, trimmed and coarsely chopped
  Coarse salt and freshly ground pepper
- 12 crostini (see page 260)
- 12 rounds (¼ inch thick) aged goat cheese, cut from a log (about 6 ounces), room temperature
  Fresh chives, snipped, for garnish

Heat 2 tablespoons oil in a skillet over medium. Cook shallot, stirring, until soft, about 3 minutes. Add mushrooms; cook, stirring occasionally, until tender and juices have evaporated, 7 to 10 minutes. Season with salt and pepper.

Top each crostini with a round of goat cheese and some mushroom mixture. Sprinkle with chives. Serve warm.

Cherry Ice

Similar to granita, this frozen dessert has a coarse, slushy texture; use a metal pan for the fastest freezing. Serves 4

- ⅓ cup dry white wine
- 2 tablespoons superfine sugar
- 2 tablespoons fresh lemon juice (from 1 lemon)
- ¼ cup water
- 2 cups fresh pitted cherries (about 12 ounces), plus whole cherries for garnish

In a bowl, whisk together wine, sugar, lemon juice, and the water to combine. Pulse cherries in a food processor until coarsely pureed. Transfer to bowl with wine mixture; stir until combined.

Pour mixture into a 9-by-13-inch baking pan and place in freezer. Stir with a fork after 20 minutes, and then stir every 10 minutes until mixture is slushy and partially solidified, about 1 hour. To serve, spoon mixture into cups; garnish with whole cherries.

{ With or without the fruit garnish, the flavor of the "ice" is revealed by its deep, inky color— cherry red. It is made even more striking by the pris- tine white bowls.

Romaine with Shallot Dressing
Chicken in Tonnato Sauce
Boiled Potatoes and Golden Beets
Cornmeal Cake with
Blueberries and Cream

PREPARATION SCHEDULE

1. Boil potatoes and beets; let cool.

2. Meanwhile, sauté shallots; bake corn cake.

3. Poach chicken; make tonnato sauce.

4. Toss potatoes and beets with thyme oil.

5. Slice chicken; assemble salad. Finish dessert just before serving.

Chicken in Tonnato Sauce

To make the sauce, buy the best-quality tuna and anchovy fillets you can find, preferably imported from Italy and packed in olive oil. The sauce can be used immediately or chilled, covered in plastic wrap, up to one day. The chicken can also be cooked up to a day ahead; let cool completely, then refrigerate. Serves 4

{ Poached chicken topped with a chilled tuna sauce is a variation on vitello (veal) tonnato, a popular Italian warm-weather dish; golden beets and potatoes are boiled, sliced, and simply finished with thyme oil and salt. For the salad course, crisp romaine is dressed with a sweet-tart dressing featuring quick-pickled shallots. Bright pink linens and tinted glass, and a smoky amethyst salt cellar, are colorful additions to the table.

2¾ pounds bone-in, skin-on chicken breast halves (about 3)
   Coarse salt and freshly ground pepper
4 cups chicken stock, homemade (see page 260) or low-sodium store-bought
1 large egg yolk
3 ounces canned tuna (⅓ cup), preferably Italian tuna packed in olive oil
2 anchovy fillets
2 tablespoons capers, preferably salt-packed, drained and rinsed
½ teaspoon finely grated lemon zest plus 2 tablespoons fresh lemon juice (from 1 lemon), plus another lemon, cut into wedges, for serving (optional)
½ cup extra-virgin olive oil

Season chicken all over with salt and pepper. Place in a 5-quart pot with stock; if necessary, add more water until chicken is completely covered. Bring to a boil over medium-high heat. Reduce heat until mixture is gently simmering, and poach until an instant-read thermometer registers 160°F, 18 to 20 minutes. Transfer to a plate and let cool completely.

Meanwhile, puree egg yolk, tuna, anchovies, capers, lemon zest and juice, and ¼ teaspoon pepper in a blender until smooth. With machine running, add oil in a slow, steady stream, blending until emulsified. If sauce is too thick, add 1 teaspoon water.

Remove skin from chicken and separate meat from the bone in one piece; discard skin and bones. Slice meat diagonally about ⅓ inch thick. Serve at room temperature or chilled, with sauce and lemon wedges, if desired.

The eggs in this recipe are not fully cooked, so it should not be prepared for pregnant women, babies, young children, the elderly, or anyone whose health is compromised.

Tender slices of golden striped beets are a lovely match for Yukon Gold potatoes. Do not substitute red beets in this recipe, as their color will bleed into the potatoes.

Boiled Potatoes and Golden Beets

To ensure even cooking, choose beets and potatoes that are similar in size. Golden beets can be found at farmers' markets and many supermarkets in the summer. Golden beets have a milder (but still sweet) flavor. Serves 4

- 1 pound Yukon Gold potatoes (about 4)
- 1 pound golden beets (about 5)
  Coarse salt
- 2 tablespoons extra-virgin olive oil
- 6 sprigs fresh thyme

Combine the potatoes and beets in a large saucepan, and cover with water by 3 inches. Bring to a boil, then reduce heat until water is at a rapid simmer. Cook until the vegetables are easily pierced with the tip of a sharp knife, about 15 minutes for the potatoes and 20 to 25 minutes for beets, transferring them to a platter with a slotted spoon as soon as each is ready. Let rest until cool enough to handle, about 10 minutes.

Use paper towels to rub the skins off the beets and a paring knife to peel the potatoes. Cut beets and potatoes into ¼-inch rounds. Arrange on a plate and season with salt.

Heat oil in a small skillet over medium; add thyme and cook until it has stopped sizzling and leaves are lightly crisped. Pour hot oil and thyme over the beets and potatoes. Serve warm or at room temperature.

Romaine with Shallot Dressing

For the dressing, finely chopped shallots are first sautéed in oil, then "pickled" with sugar and vinegar. Serves 4

- ¼ cup extra-virgin olive oil
- 3 shallots, finely chopped (about ¾ cup)
- ¼ cup red wine vinegar
- 2 teaspoons sugar
  Coarse salt and freshly ground pepper
- 2 small heads romaine, each cut into 8 wedges through the stem

Heat oil in a small skillet over medium. Sauté shallots until just starting to soften, stirring frequently, about 2 minutes. Whisk together vinegar and sugar and add to shallots; cook 1 minute, then season with salt and pepper, shaking pan well to coat shallots. Transfer shallots to a bowl and let cool completely, about 20 minutes.

Arrange romaine on four plates and top with dressing, dividing evenly. Serve immediately.

Cornmeal Cake with Blueberries and Cream

Serves 4 (with leftovers)

- 1 cup (2 sticks) plus 2 tablespoons unsalted butter, room temperature, plus more for pan
- 2 cups all-purpose flour, plus more for pan
- 1¼ cups yellow cornmeal
- 2 teaspoons baking powder
  Pinch of salt
- 1 cup sugar
- 3 large eggs, room temperature
- ½ cup sour cream
- 3 tablespoons honey
- 1 tablespoon water
- 1 cup heavy cream
- 2 cups fresh blueberries

Preheat oven to 375°F. Brush a 9-inch square baking pan with butter. Sprinkle with flour, shaking to coat evenly, then tap out excess. Whisk together flour, cornmeal, baking powder, and salt in a bowl.

With an electric mixer on medium-high speed, cream butter and ¾ cup sugar until pale and fluffy, about 3 minutes. Add eggs one at a time, beating just until incorporated after each; do not overbeat. Mix in sour cream and honey, then beat in flour mixture just until combined, scraping down sides of bowl as necessary.

Transfer batter to prepared pan, spreading smoothly with an offset spatula. Brush the surface with the water; sprinkle evenly with remaining ¼ cup sugar. Bake until cake springs back when gently pressed in the center, about 30 minutes. Cool on a wire rack.

Whip cream until soft peaks form. Cut cake into squares and split, if desired; serve with cream and berries.

How to Whip Cream

Very cold ingredients and equipment are the keys to achieving perfectly whipped cream; place the bowl and beaters (or whisk) in the freezer 10 to 15 minutes, and make sure to also chill the cream well. If you are using an electric mixer, beat on medium speed just until soft peaks form, being careful not to overbeat (which would cause the cream to turn into butter). If you are whipping the cream by hand, a large balloon whisk (so called because the wires are spread out and rounded) will work faster and more effectively than other hand-held whisks. If you wish to sweeten the cream, use confectioners' sugar, which dissolves much faster than granulated sugar. If you plan to use any flavorings, such as extracts, liqueurs, or spices, add them along with the sugar.

{ Fresh blueberries and cornmeal cake combine to make a homespun dessert that celebrates summer; other berries (or even a mixture) would work here, too. Portions are served on purple-rimmed "dinnerware" plates popular in the 1950s.

Mediterranean flavors reign in a menu that balances hot and cold as well as a range of tastes and textures: hot-off-the-grill kebabs and a chewy, crunchy pilaf share the table with a crisp, cool salad. The meal is capped off with an icy melon granita.

Pork Kebabs with Thyme
Fennel, Red Onion, and Parsley Salad
Toasted Bulgur with Almonds
Cantaloupe Granita

PREPARATION SCHEDULE

1. Make cantaloupe mixture; freeze, (scraping every 20 minutes).

2. Soak salad ingredients, then drain and dry; make bulgur side dish.

3. Grill kebabs.

4. Toss together salad.

5. Assemble dessert just before serving.

Pork Kebabs with Thyme

Lamb or chicken would also benefit from the marinade used in this recipe. If you use wooden skewers, soak them in water for thirty minutes before grilling to keep them from scorching. Serves 4

1 tablespoon finely grated orange zest
¼ cup fresh orange juice (from 1 orange)
5 garlic cloves, finely chopped
2 tablespoons coarsely chopped fresh thyme, plus sprigs for garnish
1 tablespoon Dijon mustard
Coarse salt and freshly ground pepper
¼ cup extra-virgin olive oil
1¼ pounds boneless pork loin, cut into 1½-inch cubes
Orange wedges, for serving

Whisk together orange zest and juice, garlic, thyme, mustard, 1 teaspoon salt, and ½ teaspoon pepper in a large bowl. Whisking constantly, pour in oil in a slow, steady stream; whisk until emulsified. Add pork; toss to coat. Cover bowl with plastic wrap, and let pork marinate 20 minutes at room temperature.

Heat grill to medium-high (if using a charcoal grill, coals are ready when you can hold your hand 5 inches above grill for just 3 to 4 seconds). Thread 5 or 6 cubes of pork onto each of four skewers (discard marinade); season with salt and pepper. Grill pork, turning occasionally, until cooked through and lightly charred, about 12 minutes. Garnish with thyme sprigs, and serve with orange wedges.

Fennel, Red Onion, and Parsley Salad

Soaking the main components of this simple salad in ice water renders them cool and crisp. It also helps mellow the flavor of the red onion. Serves 4

1 cup loosely packed fresh flat-leaf parsley leaves
1 fennel bulb, trimmed, halved lengthwise, and thinly sliced
1 small red onion, halved lengthwise and thinly sliced
3 tablespoons fresh lemon juice
1 tablespoon extra-virgin olive oil
½ teaspoon celery seeds
Coarse salt and freshly ground pepper

Prepare a large ice-water bath. Combine parsley, fennel, and onion in a colander, and set it in the ice-water bath. Let soak 10 to 15 minutes.

Drain mixture, and dry in a salad spinner or on paper towels. Transfer to a serving bowl. Add lemon juice, oil, and celery seeds; toss to combine. Season with salt and pepper, and serve.

Toasted Bulgur with Almonds

The bulgur in this protein- and fiber-rich side dish is toasted to bring out its deep, nutty flavor before being simmered in chicken stock. If you plan to serve the pilaf with a different main course, add a squeeze of lemon juice to the bulgur (to replace the orange from the pork). Serves 4

- 1 cup bulgur wheat
- ¾ cup chicken stock, homemade (see page 260) or low-sodium store-bought
- ¾ cup water
- 1 cinnamon stick
- 1 dried bay leaf
  Coarse salt and freshly ground pepper
- ½ cup salted roasted almonds, coarsely chopped
- 1 tablespoon extra-virgin olive oil

Heat a large skillet over medium-high. Add bulgur; toast, stirring often, until golden and fragrant, 4 to 5 minutes.

Stir together toasted bulgur, stock, the water, cinnamon stick, bay leaf, and ½ teaspoon salt in a saucepan. Bring to a boil over medium-high heat; cover, and simmer over low heat until bulgur is tender and has absorbed all liquid, 10 to 12 minutes. Discard bay leaf and cinnamon stick (or, if desired, leave in as a garnish). Stir in almonds and oil; season with salt and pepper.

Cantaloupe Granita

Look for the ripest melon you can find; it should have a sweet fragrance and a firm exterior that yields slightly at the stem end. Granita is quick to prepare, but it does take a while to reach the right consistency once it's in the freezer; you can mix it in the morning, stir and scrape it until set, then freeze in an airtight container until ready to serve. Serves 4

- 1 ripe cantaloupe (about 3 pounds), plus an additional cantaloupe, cut into wedges, for serving (optional)
- ¼ cup sugar
- 2 tablespoons fresh lemon juice
- 2 tablespoons water

Using a sharp knife, cut 1 melon in half lengthwise. Remove seeds with a spoon, and discard. Slice off and discard skin and pale green flesh. Cut melon pulp into large chunks. Puree until smooth in a food processor. Transfer to a non-reactive bowl.

Combine sugar, lemon juice, and the water in a small saucepan. Cook over medium heat until mixture has thickened slightly. Remove from heat; let cool completely.

Stir sugar syrup into melon puree to combine. Transfer to a 9-by-13-inch baking dish; place in freezer, uncovered, and stir and scrape with a fork every 20 minutes until coarse crystals form (granita should be chunky, not smooth), 1½ to 2 hours. Serve over cantaloupe wedges, if using.

With its tongue-tingling flavor and icy texture, granita is a great way to cool down after a hot summer day. For even more melon flavor, serve the granita over wedges of cantaloupe.

fall

By the time fall arrives, many of us are ready to embrace the change in weather and cooking that goes along with it. Fortunately, fall brings not only cooler days, but plentiful produce that rivals the foliage outside in its blaze of colors—from golden squash to rosy red apples— and lends itself to heartier preparations. An autumnal feast of watercress-cauliflower soup, roast pork tenderloin, and braised fennel and white beans is a good reason to turn on the oven and invite the neighbors over. There are also enticing main courses that can be quickly prepared on the stove, including pan-fried trout, skillet rib-eye steaks, sautéed chicken paillards, and pan-grilled quail. And if the change in season happens a bit later where you live, you can still use the grill to make spice-rubbed lamb chops accompanied by a corn and couscous salad. An abundance of pears, plums, grapes, figs, and other fruit makes easy work of dessert, while maple custards and dark chocolate pudding with cinnamon whipped cream offer creamy, cozy comfort in every bite.

fall menus

Everything about this dinner lends itself to being served as part of a buffet. The pork tenderloin and accompanying fennel and white bean side dish can afford to wait while everyone enjoys the soup, ladled from a stove-to-table French enameled cast-iron pot. A fruit and cheese platter completes the meal.

Watercress-Cauliflower Soup
Roasted Pork with Sage and Garlic
Braised Fennel and White Beans
Pears with Candied Walnuts and
Gorgonzola

PREPARATION SCHEDULE

1. Coat walnuts with syrup, and toast; raise oven temperature.

2. Sear pork, then roast in oven; let cheese come to room temperature.

3. Make soup; cover to keep warm.

4. Remove pork from oven; cook fennel and white beans.

5. Assemble dessert just before serving.

Watercress-Cauliflower Soup

After trimming the tough parts of the watercress stems, you should have about five cups loosely packed greens; if the bunches of watercress seem small, you may want to buy an extra, just in case. Serves 4

2   tablespoons unsalted butter
1   onion, coarsely chopped (about 1 cup)
1   small head cauliflower (about 1¾ pounds), cut into 1-inch florets
2   cups chicken stock, homemade (see page 260) or low-sodium store-bought
2   cups water
    Coarse salt and freshly ground pepper
1   bunch watercress, thick stems removed, plus small sprigs for garnish

Melt butter in a medium saucepan over medium heat. Add onion; cook, stirring occasionally, until soft and translucent, about 5 minutes. Add cauliflower, stock, the water, 2½ teaspoons salt, and ¼ teaspoon pepper. Bring to a boil. Cover, and reduce heat. Simmer, stirring once, until cauliflower is very tender when pierced with the tip of a sharp knife, about 15 minutes. Remove from heat, and stir in watercress.

Working in batches, puree soup in a blender, filling no more than halfway each time. Return soup to saucepan; cover to keep warm. To serve, ladle soup into bowls, and garnish each with a sprig of watercress and a sprinkling of pepper.

{ Thin strips of fennel and red onion are first sautéed until tender and golden before being briefly braised, along with cannellini beans; vinegar is added at the end for bright flavor, butter for richness.

Roasted Pork with Sage and Garlic

Pork tenderloin often comes in packages of two smaller ones (instead of one large, shown on page 140); in this case, simply divide the garlic mixture evenly between them, and check temperature after about fifteen minutes. The pork will continue to "cook" as it rests, so be careful not to leave it in the oven after it reaches 138 degrees. Serves 4

- 2 garlic cloves, finely chopped
- 1 tablespoon finely chopped fresh sage
  Coarse salt and freshly ground pepper
- 1 tablespoon olive oil
- 1 pork tenderloin (about 1¼ pounds), tied with kitchen twine (ask the butcher to do this for you)
- 1 tablespoon safflower or other neutral-tasting oil

Preheat oven to 400°F. Stir together garlic, sage, 1¼ teaspoons salt, ¼ teaspoon pepper, and olive oil in a small bowl. Rub mixture all over pork.

Heat a large, heavy ovenproof sauté pan over medium-high. Add safflower oil and heat until shimmering. Cook pork until seared all over, turning as each side browns, about 4 minutes total.

Transfer pan to oven. Roast pork, turning occasionally, until an instant-read thermometer inserted into thickest part registers 138°F, about 20 minutes. Transfer pork to a cutting board; tent with parchment paper, then foil, and let rest 10 minutes before slicing.

Braised Fennel and White Beans

For added flavor, prepare this dish in the same sauté pan in which the pork was cooked; remove any blackened bits with a paper towel before adding the oil. Serves 4

- 2 tablespoons extra-virgin olive oil
- 1 fennel bulb, trimmed, halved lengthwise, and cut crosswise into ¼-inch-thick slices
- 1 red onion, halved lengthwise and cut lengthwise into ¼-inch-thick slices
- 1 can (15½ ounces) cannellini beans, drained and rinsed
- 1 cup chicken stock, homemade (see page 260) or low-sodium store-bought
- 2 teaspoons coarsely chopped fresh oregano, plus whole leaves for garnish
  Coarse salt and freshly ground pepper
- 2 tablespoons red wine vinegar
- 1 tablespoon unsalted butter, room temperature

Heat oil in a large, heavy sauté pan over medium-high. Cook fennel and onion, stirring occasionally, until tender and edges are brown, about 10 minutes.

Add beans, stock, oregano, 1 teaspoon salt, and ¼ teaspoon pepper. Cook, stirring occasionally, until liquid has reduced by about half, 3 to 4 minutes. Stir in vinegar and butter; remove from heat. Garnish with oregano leaves.

Serving a Cheese Course

The harmonious flavors of cheese, nuts, and fruit (fresh or dried, or even in chutneys or jams) make a satisfying dessert course. When pairing these items, first consider the characteristics of the cheese. Stronger-flavored cheeses tend to be saltier and offer a nice contrast to sweeter fruits, such as fruit pastes, dried fruits, or very ripe fresh pears; they also pair well with roasted, salted nuts. Milder cheese, such as Brie, calls for more subtly flavored accompaniments, like fresh apples, grapes, or figs, as well as unsalted nuts. You could also choose your selection by region, since foods from the same geographic area tend to taste good together; for example, Spanish Manchego pairs beautifully with Marcona almonds and blood oranges. Other good combinations include mild goat cheese with fresh melon and pecans, or aged cheddar with dried figs and walnuts.

Pears with Candied Walnuts and Gorgonzola

Gorgonzola dolce, or dolcelatte, is a creamy, slightly sweet blue cheese. Look for it in specialty food shops and Italian markets. If you can't find it, try regular Gorgonzola, which has a richer flavor. Serves 4

- 1¼ teaspoons sugar
- ¼ teaspoon coarse salt
- 1 tablespoon unsalted butter
- 1 tablespoon pure maple syrup
- 1 cup coarsely chopped walnuts
- 4 ripe but firm Bartlett pears, preferably red, halved lengthwise, cored, and cut into wedges
- 8 ounces Gorgonzola dolce, room temperature

Preheat oven to 375°F. Stir together sugar and salt in a small bowl. Bring butter and maple syrup to a boil in a large sauté pan, then remove from heat. Add nuts, and toss to coat. Transfer nuts to a rimmed baking sheet, and sprinkle with sugar mixture; toss to coat, and spread in an even layer. Toast in oven until fragrant, about 7 minutes. Transfer sheet to a wire rack; let nuts cool completely.

To serve, arrange candied nuts, pear wedges, and cheese on a platter, with a knife for spreading cheese.

Pears have long been combined with blue cheese in salads and other dishes. Here they are served alongside candied nuts as an alternative to more traditional dessert courses. Freshly brewed espresso, with a perfect layer of froth on top, caps off the meal.

Tomato, Eggplant, and Mozzarella Stacks
Whole-Wheat Pasta with Shell Beans
Glazed Plums with Mascarpone

PREPARATION SCHEDULE

1. Toast bread crumbs for pasta.

2. Cook beans and pasta; toss together.

3. Grill eggplant; make chile oil.

4. Assemble eggplant stacks.

5. Cook plums; dollop with mascarpone just before serving.

Tomato, Eggplant, and Mozzarella Stacks

Greek oregano is more fragrant than other types of dried oregano; look for it at specialty food stores, where it is sometimes sold in bunches of dried stalks. Makes 4

- ½ large eggplant (about ½ pound), sliced crosswise into twelve ¼-inch rounds
- ¼ cup plus 2 tablespoons extra-virgin olive oil
  Coarse salt
- 2 teaspoons dried oregano, preferably Greek
- 1 teaspoon finely chopped fresh red chile (ribs and seeds removed for less heat, if desired)
- 8 to 10 ounces fresh mozzarella, sliced crosswise into twelve ¼-inch rounds
- 2 tomatoes (about ½ pound), preferably heirloom, sliced into eight ¼-inch rounds
- 12 fresh basil leaves

Heat a medium grill pan over medium. Brush eggplant slices on both sides with 3 tablespoons oil; season with salt. Working in batches, cook eggplant, turning once, until charred in places and very tender, 8 to 10 minutes total. Transfer to a platter to cool slightly.

Meanwhile, stir oregano and chopped chile with remaining 3 tablespoons oil; season with ½ teaspoon salt.

Dividing among four plates, stack eggplant, mozzarella, and tomato slices in alternating layers, finishing with tomato; tuck all but 4 basil leaves between layers and drizzle with chile oil as you go. Top each stack with a basil leaf; sprinkle with salt. Pass remaining chile oil at the table.

{ Whole-wheat pasta, given more sustenance with two types of beans, follows layered eggplant, mozzarella, and tomato starters. The seasonal vegetables (and plums in the dessert), all from the farmers' market, make this an ideal transitional menu—and hearty vegetarian meal—for late summer and early fall.

Whole-Wheat Pasta with Shell Beans

Romano beans are flat green beans that are in season in early fall; other types of pole beans (wax or green beans) may be substituted. Borlotti beans (also called cranberry beans) are plump, meaty, and flavorful; this recipe calls for jarred beans, available at Italian grocers and some supermarkets, but you can use fresh ones if you have them. Canned cannellini beans are a good alternative. Serves 4

- ¾ cup coarse fresh bread crumbs (see page 260)
- ¼ cup plus 3 tablespoons extra-virgin olive oil, plus more for drizzling
  Coarse salt and freshly ground pepper
- 1 red onion, thinly sliced
- 3 garlic cloves, coarsely chopped
- 1 teaspoon finely chopped fresh rosemary
- 8 ounces Romano beans, trimmed and cut diagonally into ¾-inch pieces
- 1½ cups jarred borlotti beans, drained and rinsed
- ¾ pound whole-wheat pasta shells, or other short pasta shape

Preheat oven to 375°F. Toss bread crumbs with 1 tablespoon oil and a pinch of salt, and spread on a rimmed baking sheet. Bake, stirring once halfway through, until golden brown and crisp, about 10 minutes.

Heat remaining ¼ cup plus 2 tablespoons olive oil in a medium skillet over medium-high. Cook onion and garlic until beginning to turn golden brown, stirring occasionally, about 4 minutes. Add rosemary and Romano beans, and season with 1½ teaspoons salt; cook, stirring often, until beans are bright in color and crisp-tender, about 4 minutes. Stir in the borlotti beans and cook until heated through, 1 to 2 minutes. Cover to keep warm.

Meanwhile, bring a large pot of water to a boil and add salt; cook pasta until al dente according to package instructions. Drain pasta, reserving about ¾ cup cooking water. Toss pasta with beans and enough reserved cooking water to coat. Season with salt and pepper.

To serve, divide pasta mixture among bowls; serve warm or at room temperature, sprinkled with bread crumbs and drizzled generously with oil.

Glazed Plums with Mascarpone

Italian prune plums are available for a few weeks in early fall. They are oblong, deep purple, and very sweet, with a texture that holds up well during cooking. Other types of plums may also be used; choose ones that are ripe but not too soft. Serve the plums with your favorite biscotti, if desired. Serves 4

- 2 tablespoons unsalted butter
- ¼ cup sugar
- 6 ripe plums, preferably Italian prune plums, halved lengthwise and pitted
- 1 tablespoon balsamic vinegar, preferably aged
- ½ cup mascarpone cheese (4 ounces), for serving

Melt butter in a medium skillet over medium heat. Sprinkle sugar evenly in pan (without stirring); when it has just begun to melt, arrange plums, cut sides down, in a single layer. Cook until plums are beginning to soften and melted sugar is bubbling, 3 to 4 minutes, reducing heat to medium-low when syrup begins to boil rapidly.

Pour vinegar into pan. Cook until plums are lightly glazed and tender but not falling apart, 3 to 5 minutes (depending on ripeness), turning plums once to coat with glaze.

Spoon plums and syrup onto four plates; dollop each with mascarpone. Serve warm.

The rims of these antique French hand-painted "fruit plates" mimic the shade of the glazed plums, while the linen napkins and contemporary serving bowls extend the color palette. A vintage tin tray is a charming way to carry the components to the table, or wherever you might wish to enjoy dessert.

Lettuce Hearts with Fried Croutons and Tomatoes
Trout with Almonds and Orange
Porcini and Parsley Farro
Sugared Grape Phyllo Tart

PREPARATION SCHEDULE

1. Prepare farro side dish.

2. Meanwhile, toast fennel seeds and layer phyllo for tart.

3. Pan-fry trout, then finish sauce.

4. Make and assemble salad.

5. Prepare and bake tart.

Trout with Almonds and Orange

Satsuma, a type of mandarin orange, has a singular sweet flavor that pairs well with the almonds, but you can use any type of orange here. You may also want to cut another orange into wedges for serving alongside the fish. Instead of buying roasted almonds, you can use blanched almonds and toast them yourself (see page 260). Serves 4

- 4 trout fillets (about 6 ounces each)
  Coarse salt and freshly ground pepper
- 3 tablespoons plus 1½ teaspoons extra-virgin olive oil
- 3 ounces roasted unsalted almonds, coarsely chopped (scant ¾ cup)
  Finely grated zest of 1 orange (2 tablespoons)
- ¼ cup plus 2 tablespoons fresh orange juice (from 1 to 2 oranges)

Pat dry fish with paper towels and season both sides with salt and pepper. Heat 2 tablespoons oil in a large skillet over medium-high until shimmering. Place 2 fillets in skillet, skin sides up. Reduce heat to medium and cook until golden underneath, 3 to 4 minutes. Carefully flip the fillets, using two spatulas if necessary. Cook until centers flake slightly when pressed, about 2 minutes more. Transfer to a platter. Repeat with 1½ teaspoons oil and remaining 2 fillets.

Wipe skillet with paper towels, and add remaining tablespoon oil and the almonds. Cook over medium heat, stirring, until almonds begin to turn golden, about 1 minute. Stir in zest, and remove from heat. Add juice and swirl to combine. To serve, place a fillet on each plate and top fish with almond mixture, dividing evenly.

Porcini and Parsley Farro

Farro, a type of hulled wheat, has been cultivated in Italy for centuries. Pearled or semi-pearled farro, which cooks more quickly than unpearled farro, is used in this recipe. Look for it at specialty food stores and Italian markets. Other grains, such as pearl barley or bulgur wheat, are good substitutions; cook them according to package instructions. Serves 4

- 2 cups farro (12 ounces)
- ¼ cup dried porcini mushrooms (about ¼ ounce), rinsed and broken into small pieces
  Coarse salt and freshly ground pepper
- 2 tablespoons plus 1 teaspoon extra-virgin olive oil
- 1 cup loosely packed fresh flat-leaf parsley leaves, coarsely chopped (⅓ cup)

Combine farro and mushrooms in a medium saucepan, and cover with cold water by 2 inches. Add 2 teaspoons salt, and bring to a boil over medium-high heat. Stir to combine, then reduce heat; simmer until farro is tender but still al dente, stirring occasionally, about 15 minutes.

Drain in a colander, then transfer farro mixture to a bowl and toss with oil and parsley. Season with 1 teaspoon salt and pepper to taste. Serve warm or at room temperature.

{ This Mediterranean-inspired meal shows how little touches add up to big flavor. Trout, quickly pan-fried on the stove, is given a last-minute "sauce" of orange zest and juice and almonds tossed together in the same pan. Porcini mushrooms add earthy flavor to farro, a nutty-tasting alternative to rice. Pan-fried croutons and ham, along with softened cherry tomatoes, embellish the salad.

Lettuce Hearts with Fried Croutons and Tomatoes

Serrano ham, a cured ham from Spain, can be found at specialty food stores; you can use prosciutto in its place. Serves 4

- 4 heads Boston lettuce, outer leaves removed, hearts split in half lengthwise
- 3 tablespoons extra-virgin olive oil
- ¼ red onion, thinly sliced
- ½ small baguette, crust removed, cut into ½-inch cubes
- 8 thin slices Serrano ham (6 ounces)
- 1 cup cherry tomatoes (5 ounces)
  Coarse salt and freshly ground pepper
- 2 tablespoons plus 1 teaspoon sherry vinegar

Arrange lettuce hearts on a serving platter. Heat a medium skillet over medium. Add 2 tablespoons oil; cook onion and bread cubes until golden brown, stirring frequently, 4 to 5 minutes. Spoon over lettuce.

Raise heat to medium-high. Lay ham slices in skillet (work in batches, if necessary). Cook until crisp, turning once, about 2 minutes; arrange slices on lettuce hearts.

Add tomatoes to skillet, tilting pan to coat with oil; cook over medium-low until soft, about 2 minutes. Season with salt and pepper. Pour in vinegar and remaining oil; let bubble briefly. Pour over lettuce, and serve.

Sugared Grape and Phyllo Tart

Unused phyllo sheets can be wrapped well in plastic and refrigerated for up to one week. Serves 4

- 1½ teaspoons fennel seeds
- 6 sheets (each 12 by 17 inches) frozen phyllo dough, thawed according to package instructions
- 6 tablespoons (¾ stick) unsalted butter, melted
- 8 teaspoons sugar
- 1 cup red seedless grapes (6 ounces)

Preheat oven to 400°F. Toast fennel seeds in a skillet over medium heat, shaking pan occasionally, until fragrant, about 1 minute. Transfer to a cutting board and let cool 3 minutes, then crush coarsely with the side of a knife.

Trim phyllo sheets into 10-by-12-inch rectangles. Lay one rectangle on a baking sheet (keep remaining sheets covered); brush entire surface lightly with butter. Sprinkle evenly with 1 teaspoon sugar and ¼ teaspoon fennel seeds. Top with another phyllo sheet. Repeat four times, ending with last phyllo sheet. (Keep covered with a damp towel.)

Arrange grapes on top. Brush with remaining butter; sprinkle with remaining 2 teaspoons sugar. Bake until crisp and golden, 13 to 15 minutes. Transfer to a wire rack to cool slightly before cutting into squares. Serve warm.

A large grape-studded tart is cut into small squares for serving; the transferware pattern on the plate brings a vineyard to mind. A rich, raisiny dessert wine, such as amontillado (a medium-dry sherry) or Madeira pairs well with the fruit dessert; here the wine is served in assorted etched glasses—some footed, others not.

An early fall menu featuring Indian flavors makes good use of end-of-season corn and tomatoes, and of okra at its peak. The couscous salad can be prepared while the grill is heating, the okra once the lamb has come off the grill.

Grilled Spiced Lamb Chops
Corn and Couscous Salad
Sautéed Okra and Tomatoes
Papaya with Coconut-Lime Yogurt

PREPARATION SCHEDULE

1. Heat grill; rub lamb with spice mixture and let rest.

2. Meanwhile, prepare couscous salad; toast coconut for dessert.

3. Grill lamb chops.

4. Sauté okra and tomatoes.

5. After dinner, assemble dessert.

Grilled Spiced Lamb Chops

Garam masala is an Indian spice blend available in specialty stores and some supermarkets. To make your own, mix together one-half teaspoon each of ground black pepper, cinnamon, cardamom, cumin, and coriander, along with a generous pinch of ground cloves. You can use a grill pan instead of a grill to cook the chops. Serves 4

2 teaspoons garam masala
2 teaspoons coarse salt
1 teaspoon freshly ground pepper
4 lamb shoulder chops (each 6 to 7 ounces and ¾ inch thick)
  Olive oil, for brushing grill
  Cilantro sprigs, for garnish

Heat grill to medium-high (if using a charcoal grill, coals are ready when you can hold your hand 5 inches above grill for just 3 to 4 seconds). Combine garam masala, salt, and pepper in a small bowl. Place lamb chops on a baking sheet, pat dry with paper towels, and rub both sides with equal amounts of spice mixture. Let sit at room temperature 20 minutes.

Lightly oil grates. Grill chops until they reach desired doneness, about 4 minutes on the first side and 3 to 4 minutes on the second side for medium-rare. Transfer to a platter, and garnish with cilantro.

Corn and Couscous Salad

The couscous is "cooked" by combining with boiling water (off heat) and letting it steam, covered. Serves 4

1 teaspoon curry powder, preferably Madras
2 teaspoons coarse-grain mustard
1 tablespoon plus 1 teaspoon white wine vinegar
  Coarse salt and freshly ground pepper
3 tablespoons extra-virgin olive oil
¾ cup couscous
1 cup boiling water
1 Vidalia or other sweet onion, diced (1 cup)
3 garlic cloves, minced
1 fresh red chile, minced (optional; ribs and seeds removed for less heat, if desired)
3 cups fresh corn kernels (cut from about 4 ears)
¼ cup finely chopped cilantro

In a medium bowl, whisk together curry powder, mustard, and vinegar. Season with salt and pepper. While whisking, slowly drizzle in 2 tablespoons oil; whisk until emulsified.

Place couscous in a bowl. Pour the boiling water over couscous; stir just to combine. Cover with a plate; let steam until water is absorbed, about 5 minutes. Fluff with a fork.

Heat the remaining tablespoon oil in a large skillet over medium-high. Cook onion, stirring occasionally, until softened, about 4 minutes. Stir in garlic and chile (if using); cook, stirring, until softened, about 2 minutes. Add corn; cook until just tender, about 2 minutes.

Stir corn mixture into couscous. Add curry vinaigrette and cilantro; toss to combine. Season with salt and pepper. Serve warm or at room temperature.

Sautéed Okra and Tomatoes

Fresh okra is available in the fall and spring. Smaller pods are generally more tender than larger ones. Frozen (and thawed) okra can be used in a pinch. Serves 4

- 1 tablespoon yellow mustard seeds
- ½ teaspoon cumin seeds
- ½ teaspoon ground coriander
- 2 tablespoons extra-virgin olive oil
- 1 small red onion, cut lengthwise into ½-inch-thick wedges
  - Coarse salt and freshly ground pepper
- 1 pound fresh okra, stems trimmed
- ¼ cup water, plus more if needed
- 3 tomatoes, seeded and cut into ½-inch-thick wedges

Combine mustard and cumin seeds with coriander. Heat oil in a large skillet over medium. Cook onion with a pinch of salt, stirring, until soft, about 3 minutes.

Raise heat to medium-high; add spice mixture, okra, and the water. Cook, stirring, until okra is bright green and just tender, about 6 minutes, adding more water if skillet becomes too dry.

Add tomato wedges; cook until just heated through, 1 minute. Season with salt and pepper. Serve immediately.

Papaya with Coconut-Lime Yogurt

Papayas are ripe when they are slightly soft to the touch. To speed up ripening, place papayas near fruits that produce ethylene gas, such as bananas. Mango would also work well in this recipe. Serves 4

- ¼ cup shredded sweetened coconut
- 1 container (7 ounces) Greek-style plain yogurt
- 1 tablespoon honey
- 1 tablespoon fresh lime juice, plus lime wedges for serving
- 1 large or 3 small ripe papayas, peeled, halved lengthwise, and seeded

Spread coconut evenly over bottom of a small skillet, and cook over medium heat, tossing occasionally, until just golden, about 2 minutes. Transfer to a plate; let cool completely.

Save some toasted coconut for garnishing, if desired, and whisk together the rest in a bowl with the yogurt, honey, and lime juice. Slice papaya into 1-inch-thick wedges. Serve papaya with yogurt mixture (garnished with reserved coconut, if desired) and lime wedges on the side.

A melon-hued tablecloth brilliantly harmonizes with the color of the papaya in this refreshing dessert. To serve, squeeze the lime wedges over the papaya; the accompanying yogurt sauce can be used for dipping, or spooned over the plated wedges.

This meal begins and ends with bite-size dishes that can be nibbled at or away from the table. And although they could be served on their own, chicken paillards taste even better over a salad of arugula and roasted sweet potatoes; the warm walnut sauce slightly wilts the peppery greens.

Chickpea-Olive Crostini
Chicken Paillards with Walnut Sauce
Arugula and Roasted Sweet-Potato Salad
Goat Cheese–Stuffed Dates

PREPARATION SCHEDULE

1. Roast sweet potatoes and reduce oven temperature; make vinaigrette.

2. Bake crostini, and make topping; prepare dessert.

3. Assemble crostini; serve.

4. Cook chicken; make sauce.

5. Toss salad just before serving.

Chicken Paillards with Walnut Sauce

If the cutlets are thicker than one-quarter inch, or vary in thickness, place them between pieces of plastic wrap and pound with a meat mallet to help them cook evenly. Serves 4

- 3 tablespoons safflower or other neutral-tasting oil
- 4 chicken cutlets (each 4 to 6 ounces and ¼ inch thick)
  Coarse salt and freshly ground pepper
- ⅓ cup walnut halves
- ½ cup chicken stock, homemade (see page 260) or low-sodium store-bought
- 2 tablespoons sherry vinegar
  Arugula and Roasted Sweet-Potato Salad

Heat oil in a large sauté pan over medium-high until hot but not smoking. Pat dry chicken and season both sides with salt and pepper, then place in the pan (cook in batches, if necessary, to avoid crowding). Cook until golden brown on first side, 3 to 4 minutes; turn chicken and continue cooking until golden on the other side and cooked through, 2 to 3 minutes. Transfer to a platter.

Reduce heat to medium-low. Add walnuts and toast, stirring constantly, until golden, about 3 minutes. Raise heat to medium; add stock and vinegar. Cook, swirling the pan, until liquid is reduced by half and slightly thickened, about 1 minute.

To serve, divide the salad evenly among plates, and top with chicken; pour sauce over chicken.

Arugula and Roasted Sweet-Potato Salad

This room-temperature salad can be made with other seasonal vegetables instead of the sweet potatoes. Try using winter squash, beets, or parsnips, peeled and cut into uniform pieces so they will cook evenly. Serves 4

- 2 sweet potatoes (about 8 ounces each), cut into 1-inch-thick rounds or half-moons (unpeeled)
- 2 leeks, white and pale-green parts only, halved lengthwise and cut into 2-inch pieces, washed well (see page 260)
- ¼ cup extra-virgin olive oil
  Coarse salt and freshly ground pepper
- 1½ teaspoons Dijon mustard
- 1 tablespoon sherry vinegar
- 4 cups loosely packed baby arugula (about 5 ounces), washed well and dried

Preheat oven to 400°F. Combine sweet potatoes and leeks on a rimmed baking sheet, and toss with 2 tablespoons oil; season with 1 teaspoon salt and a pinch of pepper. Spread in a single layer and roast until leeks are golden and sweet potatoes are tender when pierced with a fork, 20 to 22 minutes, tossing once halfway through. Let cool about 10 minutes.

Meanwhile, whisk together mustard and vinegar, then slowly whisk in remaining 2 tablespoons oil; season with salt and pepper.

Toss roasted vegetables with arugula and vinaigrette.

Chickpea-Olive Crostini

Serves 4

- ¼ cup extra-virgin olive oil
- 2 large garlic cloves, coarsely chopped (2 tablespoons)
- ½ red onion, finely chopped (¾ cup)
- ¼ teaspoon crushed red-pepper flakes
- ¼ teaspoon ground cumin
- 1¼ cups drained and rinsed canned chickpeas
- 6 oil-cured black olives, pitted and coarsely chopped
- 2 tablespoons coarsely chopped fresh flat-leaf parsley
- 16 crostini (see page 260)
  Coarse salt

Heat 3 tablespoons oil in a medium skillet over medium-high. Cook garlic, onion, and red-pepper flakes, stirring occasionally, until lightly golden and fragrant, about 4 minutes. Stir in the cumin and chickpeas; cook, tossing, until warmed through, about 2 minutes. Transfer to a bowl. Using a fork or wooden spoon, coarsely mash chickpeas. Stir in olives and parsley; season with salt.

To serve, spoon a heaping tablespoon of chickpea mixture onto each crostini; drizzle with remaining tablespoon oil.

Goat Cheese–Stuffed Dates

Medjool dates are large and plump, with a wonderfully sweet taste. They are widely available, but other types of dates can be substituted (as long as they are moist). Serves 4

- ¼ cup fresh goat cheese (about 2 ounces), softened
- 2 tablespoons heavy cream
- 12 large Medjool dates
  Coarse sea salt, such as fleur de sel or Maldon, for sprinkling

Beat goat cheese by hand until smooth, then stir in heavy cream until the mixture is smooth and spreadable.

Make a slit lengthwise in each date, and remove the pit. Fill each date with a heaping teaspoon of goat-cheese mixture. Sprinkle with salt just before serving.

Made with just four ingredients, stuffed dates are an effortless ending to almost any meal. Here the dates are served on an antique English transferware plate, with glasses of tawny port on the side.

A casual steak dinner is right at home on a simply set table, accompanied by a robust red wine, such as Chianti, or hearty ale; a loaf of rustic bread would also be welcome. Rib-eye is exceptionally moist and tender, so it's a good choice for entertaining; molten chocolate cakes with a touch of ground espresso provide a memorable ending.

Skillet Rib-Eye Steaks
Broiled Peppers with Melted Cheese
Broccoli with Garlic and Anchovies
Molten Chocolate-Espresso Cakes

PREPARATION SCHEDULE

1. Season steaks and bring to room temperature.

2. Meanwhile, mix batter and bake cakes.

3. Cook broccoli.

4. Sear steaks.

5. Broil peppers while steaks rest.

Skillet Rib-Eye Steaks

When cooking the steaks, place them in the pan side by side, with room between (or cook one at a time); this will ensure that they sear properly and form a nice crust. Serves 4

- 2 bone-in rib-eye steaks (about 1 pound each)
   Coarse salt and freshly ground pepper
- ⅓ cup loosely packed small rosemary sprigs, leaves picked from stems and coarsely chopped (¼ cup)
- 2 tablespoons extra-virgin olive oil
- 2 garlic cloves

Place steaks on a plate and pat dry with paper towels; season both sides generously with salt and pepper. Reserve half the rosemary; sprinkle the remaining evenly over top of each steak, pressing to adhere. Let come to room temperature, 20 to 30 minutes.

Heat a large cast-iron skillet over medium, then add oil and garlic. When oil is hot but not smoking, push garlic to the edge of pan and add steaks, rosemary side up. Cook steaks until a dark-brown crust forms on the bottom, about 5 minutes. Turn with tongs and cook 3 to 4 minutes more for medium-rare (remove garlic once it begins to turn brown). Transfer steaks to a cutting board to rest 5 minutes.

Meanwhile, add reserved rosemary to the skillet; once it begins to sizzle, stir to coat with the oil and, tilting skillet to collect oil, spoon it over the steaks. Slice steaks by cutting parallel to the bone on the diagonal.

Broiled Peppers with Melted Cheese

Choose peppers according to availability and preference; Italian frying peppers, Anaheim chiles, and bell peppers are good options. Keeping the stems intact, split thin, long peppers in half—retain seeds of spicy chiles if more heat is desired—or quarter larger bell peppers lengthwise. Instead of Asiago, try other good melting cheeses, such as provolone or mozzarella. Serves 4

- 4 fresh peppers, halved lengthwise through stem (or quartered if large), seeds removed
- 4 ounces Asiago cheese, thinly sliced

Heat broiler, with rack about 6 inches from heat source. Place halved peppers, cut sides up, on a baking sheet. Broil until beginning to soften, about 6 minutes.

Remove from broiler; drape cheese over each pepper piece. Continue broiling until cheese is melted and bubbling and pepper is blackened around edges, 2 to 3 minutes. Let cool slightly before serving.

Broccoli with Garlic and Anchovies

Don't be put off by the number of anchovies in this recipe; they will soften and mellow during cooking, contributing wonderful flavor without being the least bit overpowering. Serves 4

- 2 tablespoons extra-virgin olive oil
- 1 large head broccoli (1¼ pounds), trimmed and cut lengthwise through stalk into long spears (4 to 6 inches long)
- 1 garlic clove, coarsely chopped
- 6 anchovy fillets, coarsely chopped
  Coarse salt and freshly ground pepper
- ¼ cup water
- 1 tablespoon balsamic vinegar

Heat oil in a large, heavy skillet over medium until hot but not smoking. Add broccoli (in a single layer, if possible), and cook, without turning, until bottom sides are nicely browned, 3 to 4 minutes.

Add garlic and anchovies, and season with a pinch each of salt and pepper; flip broccoli pieces. Cook, stirring, until garlic and anchovies are fragrant, 1 to 2 minutes. Add the water, and continue cooking until broccoli is just tender (the stalk should provide little resistance when pierced with the tip of a sharp knife), 5 to 6 minutes.

Remove from heat. Season with more pepper, and add vinegar to pan, stirring to coat broccoli. Serve hot.

Molten Chocolate-Espresso Cakes

Makes 6

- 4 tablespoons (½ stick) unsalted butter, room temperature, plus more for tin
- ⅓ cup sugar, plus more for tin
- 8 ounces bittersweet chocolate, coarsely chopped
- ⅓ cup all-purpose flour
- 1 tablespoon instant espresso powder
- ¼ teaspoon salt
- 3 large eggs
- 1 teaspoon pure vanilla extract

Preheat oven to 400°F. Brush 6 cups of a standard muffin tin with butter, and dust with sugar; tap out excess. Melt chocolate in a heatproof bowl set over (not in) a pan of simmering water, stirring until smooth. Let chocolate cool.

Whisk together flour, espresso powder, and salt. With an electric mixer on medium-high, beat butter and sugar until light and fluffy. Add eggs one at a time, mixing until completely incorporated after each. Add flour mixture, and beat until combined. Beat in vanilla and chocolate.

Spoon batter into prepared cups, dividing evenly. Bake until cakes no longer jiggle when tin is shaken, 8 to 10 minutes. Transfer to a wire rack to cool at least 10 minutes before turning out cakes.

Freshly brewed espresso, served trattoria-style in short glasses, complements the mini cakes' deep chocolate flavor (and hint of espresso). Served warm, their centers are very soft. When cooled to room temperature, they become dense and fudgelike.

Black-eyed peas, Monterey Jack cheese, and pumpkin seeds all contribute protein—and Southwestern flavor—to this vegetarian meal. Roasted vegetables lend depth to the pumpkin soup, and cilantro brightens the filling for the flautas. Each dish is delicious without being too heavy, leaving plenty of room for the scrumptious apple crumble.

Roasted Pumpkin Soup
Cheese Flautas with Cilantro Pesto
Black-Eyed Pea Salad with Baby Greens
Apple-Cranberry Crumble

PREPARATION SCHEDULE

1. Roast the vegetables for the soup; meanwhile, prepare pesto.

2. Bake crumble; toss black-eyed peas for salad.

3. Form flautas; cover with a damp towel.

4. Puree soup and keep hot.

5. Fry flautas and add greens to salad just before serving.

Cheese Flautas with Cilantro Pesto

This Mexican-style pesto is made with pepitas (hulled green pumpkin seeds) instead of nuts; look for them at natural-food stores, gourmet grocers, or Latin markets. Serves 4

¼ cup extra-virgin olive oil
2 garlic cloves, thinly sliced
¾ cup pepitas
1 cup loosely packed cilantro leaves, chopped
   Juice of 1 lime (2 tablespoons)
   Coarse salt and freshly ground pepper
8 corn tortillas (6-inch)
2 cups grated Monterey Jack cheese (6 ounces)
¼ cup peanut oil

Heat 2 tablespoons olive oil in a medium sauté pan over medium-low. Cook garlic, swirling pan, until golden, 1 to 2 minutes. Add pepitas; cook, tossing, until lightly toasted, 2 to 3 minutes. Transfer to a food processor; pulse to a coarse puree. Add cilantro, lime juice, and remaining 2 tablespoons olive oil; pulse until smooth. Season pesto with salt and pepper.

To soften tortillas, dip one at a time in water and use tongs to heat over the flame of a gas burner until pliable, turning once, 15 to 20 seconds per side. (Alternatively, wrap wet tortillas in a kitchen towel; microwave 15 to 20 seconds.)

To assemble, spread cilantro pesto down middle of each tortilla; top with cheese. Roll up to enclose filling; place seam side down as you work. Keep covered with a damp kitchen towel if not frying immediately.

Heat the peanut oil in a medium skillet over medium until shimmering. Working in two batches, place flautas seam sides down in skillet; fry until first side is golden, about 1 minute. Using tongs, begin slowly rolling flautas in the oil to brown evenly, cooking for about 1 minute more. Transfer to paper towels to drain, dabbing the tops to remove excess oil. Serve immediately.

Black-Eyed Pea Salad with Baby Greens

Baby spinach and red mustard leaves are more tender and spicy than the familiar varieties of those greens. You can use other spicy baby lettuces, such as chard and tatsoi, or look for packaged blends (sometimes called spring or Asian mix) in many supermarkets. Serves 4

- 1 can (15 ounces) black-eyed peas, drained and rinsed
- 1 tomato, diced (¾ cup)
- ½ large red onion, thinly sliced
- 1 garlic clove, minced
- 1 tablespoon coarsely chopped cilantro
- 1 tablespoon red wine vinegar
- 1 teaspoon Dijon mustard
- 3 tablespoons extra-virgin olive oil
   Coarse salt and freshly ground pepper
- 6 cups baby spinach
- 2 cups baby red mustard greens

In a large bowl, gently toss black-eyed peas with tomato, onion, garlic, cilantro, vinegar, mustard, and oil; season with salt and pepper.

When ready to serve, combine spinach and mustard greens in a large salad bowl. Top with the bean salad, and gently toss to combine.

Roasted Pumpkin Soup

Instead of sugar pumpkins, you can use other winter squash. Kabocha, calabaza, and Hubbard are the best alternatives. Choose a squash that feels heavy for its size and is free of soft spots. The soup can be garnished with toasted pepitas or a dollop of sour cream—or both. Serves 4

- 2¾ pounds sugar pumpkin, stemmed, halved lengthwise, seeds removed
- 1 onion, peeled and quartered through the stem
- 2 shiitake mushrooms, stemmed, caps wiped clean with a damp paper towel
- 1 garlic clove, peeled
- ½ cup olive oil
   Coarse salt and freshly ground pepper
- 5 cups vegetable stock, homemade (see page 261) or low-sodium store-bought

Preheat oven to 450°F. Cut pumpkin into 2-inch pieces. Combine pumpkin, onion, mushrooms, and garlic on a large rimmed baking sheet. Add the oil and 2 teaspoons salt; toss to coat, then spread in a single layer. Roast until pumpkin pieces are tender when pierced with the tip of a sharp knife, about 30 minutes, rotating pan and tossing vegetables halfway through. When pumpkin pieces are cool enough to handle, remove skin.

Transfer vegetables to a 4-quart saucepan and set over medium heat. Pour in 2 cups of stock, then puree with an immersion blender until smooth. With the blender running, slowly add the remaining 3 cups stock, and puree until smooth. (To use a regular blender, first combine all of the stock with vegetables in the pot, and then transfer to blender in batches, being careful not to fill more than halfway.) Bring soup just to a simmer. Remove from heat, and season with salt and pepper. Cover to keep warm until ready to serve.

Apple-Cranberry Crumble

Honeycrisp apples have a firm texture that holds up well during baking; Macoun, Empire, or Fuji are other good choices. Fresh (or frozen) cranberries contribute flavor as well as some juice; do not substitute dried cranberries. A mini-chopper makes quick work of chopping the cranberries. Serves 4

For filling
- 1½ pounds apples (about 3 medium), peeled and cored
- ½ cup fresh or frozen (unthawed) cranberries, coarsely chopped
- ¼ cup granulated sugar
- ½ teaspoon ground cinnamon
   Pinch of salt

For topping
- 4 tablespoons (½ stick) cold unsalted butter, cut into small pieces, plus more, room temperature, for baking dish
- ½ cup pecan halves (2 ounces), coarsely chopped
- ¼ cup all-purpose flour
- ¼ cup old-fashioned rolled oats (not quick-cooking)
- 3 tablespoons packed light-brown sugar
   Pinch of salt
   Sour cream, for serving (optional)

Preheat oven to 425°F. Prepare filling: Quarter apples lengthwise, then thinly slice. Toss in a large bowl with remaining filling ingredients until evenly coated.

Prepare topping: Butter an 8-inch square glass or ceramic baking dish. Mix pecans, flour, oats, brown sugar, and salt in a bowl until combined. Work in butter with your fingertips until mixture is crumbly, with pea-size chunks.

Spread filling in prepared baking dish and sprinkle evenly with topping. Bake until filling is bubbling and topping is crisp and golden brown, 25 to 30 minutes. Let cool slightly before serving, dolloped with sour cream, if desired.

Two types of fruit—cranberries and apples—are better than one in this pecan-and-oat-topped crumble. For a nice bit of tang and creaminess, dollop some sour cream into each serving.

Broiling is an expedient way to cook fish; a miso glaze is brushed on first for flavor and color. Wilted cabbage with ginger and garlic, along with toasted sesame seeds, turns brown rice into a delicious side dish. Chopsticks are an authentic choice for the Japanese-inspired menu, as are glasses of chilled sake.

Tofu and Scallions in Mushroom Broth
Miso-Glazed Fish Fillets
Sesame Brown Rice and Cabbage
Caramelized Persimmons

PREPARATION SCHEDULE

1. Cook cabbage and rice, then toss together.
2. Meanwhile, make mushroom broth.
3. Broil fish, and cover to keep warm.
4. Garnish broth with tofu and scallions.
5. Broil persimmons, and make lime mascarpone just before serving.

Miso-Glazed Fish Fillets

Miso is a fermented soybean paste. The lighter, or "white," version is milder and less salty than brown miso, and is sometimes referred to as sweet miso. It can be found in the Asian section of many supermarkets and most health-food stores. Black cod is actually not a true cod, but rather a type of sable-fish that is often called butterfish (because of its high oil content). With its rich flavor and velvety texture, black cod is the best choice for this dish, but other firm white-flesh fish, such as halibut or Arctic char, can be used instead. Serves 4

- 2 tablespoons mirin (Japanese sweet rice cooking wine)
- 2 tablespoons rice wine vinegar (unseasoned)
- ⅓ cup white (shiro) miso
- 2 tablespoons sugar
  Safflower or other neutral-tasting oil, for baking sheet
- 4 skinless black cod fillets (6 ounces each)

Combine mirin, vinegar, miso, and sugar in a small sauce-pan. Whisking constantly, cook over medium heat until sugar has dissolved. Remove from heat; transfer glaze to a small bowl and let cool completely.

Heat broiler, with rack 6 inches from heat source. Coat a baking sheet lightly with oil. Arrange fish on sheet, and brush generously with miso glaze. Broil until fillets are browned on top and opaque throughout, 6 to 8 minutes. (If tops brown before fish is cooked through, cover loosely with foil.) Serve warm.

Sesame Brown Rice and Cabbage

Toasting the grains before adding the water gives the rice a subtle nutty flavor. Toasting the sesame seeds has the same effect; for instructions, see page 260. Serves 4

- 2 tablespoons safflower or other neutral-tasting oil
- 1 cup coarsely chopped napa cabbage (¼ head)
- 2 teaspoons peeled and minced fresh ginger
- 1 small garlic clove, minced
- 1 cup long-grain brown rice
  Coarse salt
- 1½ cups water
- 2 teaspoons rice wine vinegar (unseasoned)
- 1 tablespoon sesame seeds

Heat the oil in a 4-quart saucepan with a tight-fitting lid over medium. Add cabbage, ginger, and garlic; cook (uncovered), stirring often, until cabbage is wilted, about 2 minutes. Spoon cabbage mixture onto a plate.

Add rice to the pan, and stir to coat with the oil; cook, stirring, until lightly toasted, about 1 minute. Add 1 teaspoon salt and the water; bring to a boil, then reduce heat to low. Cover and cook 30 minutes. Remove from heat and let sit, covered, 5 minutes. Fluff with a fork, then add cabbage mixture, vinegar, and sesame seeds, and toss to combine.

Tofu and Scallions in Mushroom Broth

This simple broth is served in small bowls as an appetizer, similar to miso soup. The mushrooms are used only to flavor the broth, while tofu provides a little substance. Look for dried shiitake mushrooms in specialty food stores and many super- markets. Serves 4

- 1 ounce dried shiitake mushrooms (1 cup)
- 4 cups water
- 1 tablespoon soy sauce, preferably tamari
- ½ teaspoon rice wine vinegar (unseasoned)
- 2 ounces firm tofu, cut into ¼-inch cubes (¼ cup)
- 1 scallion, green part only, sliced very thin, for garnish

Combine mushrooms and the water in a small saucepan, and bring to a boil over high heat. Reduce heat until liquid is at a simmer; cook, partially covered, until broth is a rich brown color, about 25 minutes.

Strain mixture through a fine sieve into a medium bowl (or large liquid measuring cup), pressing on mushrooms with a wooden spoon to remove as much liquid as possible; discard mushrooms. Stir soy sauce and vinegar into broth; divide evenly among four bowls. Add tofu, and garnish with scallion. Serve immediately.

Caramelized Persimmons

Fuyu persimmons have a glossy red-orange skin, a squat, round shape (similar to a tomato), and a tangy-sweet flavor. They are available from September through December at farmers' markets, Asian grocers, and some supermarkets. Choose fruit that is ripe but still slightly firm. Serves 4

- 4 ripe Fuyu persimmons
- 3 tablespoons honey
- 2 tablespoons fresh lime juice (from 1 to 2 limes)
- 9 ounces mascarpone cheese (about 1 cup)
- 1 teaspoon pure vanilla extract
     Chopped candied ginger, for garnish (optional)

Heat broiler, with rack 6 inches from heat source. Slice persimmons in half crosswise. Place halves cut side up in a baking dish, and drizzle each half with honey. Broil until golden brown and caramelized, 6 to 8 minutes. Remove from oven; immediately sprinkle 1 tablespoon lime juice over fruit.

While fruit is broiling, whisk together mascarpone, vanilla, and remaining tablespoon lime juice.

To serve, dollop each persimmon half with mascarpone mixture; sprinkle with candied ginger or sugar, if desired.

{ Topped with mascarpone cheese flavored with lime and vanilla, caramelized persimmons make a luscious yet not too heavy dessert. Candied ginger is a delicious (though optional) garnish.

Gratinéed Baked Squash Halves
Quail with Figs and Pine Nuts
Classic Rice Pilaf
Frozen Grapes with Sauternes Granita

PREPARATION SCHEDULE

1. Make granita; freeze.
2. Roast squash.
3. Meanwhile, make rice pilaf.
4. Remove squash from oven; raise oven temperature.
5. Roast figs and cook quail.

Quail with Figs and Pine Nuts

This recipe calls for "bone-out" quail with only the leg bones intact, available at many butchers and specialty food stores. If you can only find bone-in quail, you will need to remove the backbone (called spatchcocking) to allow the bird to cook evenly: Use kitchen shears to cut along both sides of the backbone from tail to neck to remove, keeping the bird intact (discard backbone, or save to make stock), then press down on the breast to flatten quail. If the feet are still attached, use shears to cut them off. Serves 4

- 3 tablespoons olive oil
- 20 fresh Black Mission figs, halved lengthwise
  Coarse salt and freshly ground pepper
- ¼ cup pine nuts
- 2 tablespoons capers, preferably salt-packed, drained and rinsed
- ¼ cup good-quality balsamic vinegar
- 8 fresh bone-out quail (about 4 ounces each), feet removed
  Classic Rice Pilaf (recipe follows)

Preheat oven to 450°F. Pour the oil onto a rimmed baking sheet, and tilt to coat evenly. Place figs on sheet, cut sides up; season with salt and pepper. Roast 10 minutes. Sprinkle pine nuts and capers into pan, and gently shake pan to coat them with oil. Roast 5 minutes. Remove from oven. Pour in vinegar, and stir to incorporate the browned bits from the bottom of the pan. Transfer mixture to a plate to cool slightly.

While figs are roasting, heat a grill pan over medium-high for 5 minutes. Using paper towels, pat dry quail; season both sides with salt and pepper. When pan is hot, brush lightly with oil. Working in batches to avoid crowding, add the quail, back sides down. Place a cast-iron skillet or other heavy pan on top and weight with a heavy object (such as canned goods or another skillet). Cook until browned and slightly crisped on first side, about 4 minutes (3 minutes for later batches). Turn quail with tongs and continue cooking, without the weight, until golden brown on the other side, 3 to 4 minutes more (2 minutes for later batches). Transfer each batch to a platter; tent with parchment paper, then foil, to keep warm.

To serve, divide rice pilaf among four plates and place quail on top; spoon fig mixture over and around each.

Quail is often reserved for entertaining, yet the tiny birds are so quick to prepare, they can be served any time. In this casual yet impressive meal—which begins with baked acorn squash and ends with wine-flavored granita—the quail are served over rice pilaf and accompanied by roasted figs, pine nuts, and capers.

Classic Rice Pilaf

Dried angel hair pasta, or capellini, adds textural contrast to the rice in this pilaf. Vermicelli, which has even thinner strands, would be a fine substitute. Serves 4

2 tablespoons unsalted butter
¼ cup broken (1-inch pieces) angel hair pasta
½ yellow onion, cut into small dice (¾ cup)
1 cup long-grain white rice
Coarse salt
1½ cups water

Melt butter in a 2-quart saucepan with a tight-fitting lid over medium heat. Add pasta, and stir to coat with butter; cook (uncovered), stirring, until golden, about 2 minutes. Add onion; cook, stirring frequently, until translucent, about 4 minutes. Add rice, stirring to coat evenly with butter, then add 1 teaspoon salt.

Pour in the water and bring to a boil; stir once. Cover, and reduce heat to medium low. Simmer until rice has absorbed all the liquid, about 15 minutes. Remove from heat; let sit, covered, 5 minutes. Fluff with a fork and serve.

Gratinéed Baked Squash Halves

If the squash halves do not sit upright in the baking dish, slice off the pointy tips and stems to make flat. Other fresh herbs, especially thyme, can also be used to infuse the cream (discard large leaves and sprigs before serving, if desired). Serves 4

2 acorn squash, halved crosswise, seeds removed
Coarse salt and freshly ground pepper
½ cup heavy cream
8 fresh sage leaves, torn in half
2 garlic cloves, thinly sliced
½ cup grated Gruyère cheese (about 2 ounces)

Preheat oven to 375°F. Place squash halves, cut sides up, in a 9-inch baking dish. Season with salt and pepper. Pour about ½ cup water into baking dish around squash.

Combine cream with sage and garlic in a small saucepan, and bring to a simmer over medium-high heat. Pour into squash halves, dividing evenly.

Bake until squash are tender when pierced with the tip of a sharp knife, 30 to 40 minutes. Remove from oven; sprinkle with cheese, dividing evenly. Continue baking until cheese is melted and golden, about 10 minutes. Serve hot.

Baked squash becomes a rich and luscious first course when filled with heavy cream flavored with sage and garlic and finished with melted cheese.

Dessert Wines

Wines best suited for dessert are, almost without exception, those that retain some of the grape's natural sweetness. These include fortified wines, such as sherry, port, and Madeira, and "late-harvest" wines (so called because they are made from grapes left on the vine for more time than usual, which increases their sweetness). Some late-harvest wines, such as riesling and gewürztraminer, are labeled as such, while others—including French Sauternes, one of the more elegant options—are not. Italian sparkling dessert wines, such as Moscato and Spumanti, are refreshing and widely available.

A little sweet wine goes a long way, so purchase half-bottles whenever possible (opened bottles will keep a few days longer than non-dessert wines). To fully appreciate their flavors, serve dessert wines just slightly cooler than room temperature.

Frozen Grapes with Sauternes Granita

This granita has a slushy consistency. For a coarser texture that's similar to shaved ice, freeze the granita for a total of four hours, scraping it with a fork every thirty minutes. Serves 4

- 10 ounces red seedless grapes (about 2 cups)
- 3 tablespoons Sauternes
- 1 tablespoon water
- 1 tablespoon sugar

Cut about half of the grapes in half. Spread all of the grapes in an 8-inch square baking dish. Pour Sauternes and water over grapes, and sprinkle evenly with sugar.

Freeze until liquid has started to crystallize on the top and at the edges, about 1 hour. To serve, scrape granita with fork tines, and transfer to individual glasses.

A French dessert wine and seedless grapes are used to make an especially easy granita, which requires only an hour in the freezer (and no stirring) before being scraped into serving glasses.

Roasted Parsnip and Chorizo Bites
Steamed Mussels and Clams in Smoky Tomato Broth
Orange and Endive Salad
Dark Chocolate Puddings

PREPARATION SCHEDULE

1. Make pudding and refrigerate; soak mussels and clams.

2. Roast parsnips and chorizo; assemble salad.

3. Assemble chorizo bites, and serve.

4. Steam mussels and clams.

5. Make whipped cream just before serving dessert.

Steamed Mussels and Clams in Smoky Tomato Broth

Pimentón, or smoked paprika, is a staple of Spanish cooking. It is available hot or sweet (depending on your taste preference), and can be found at specialty food stores and some supermarkets. Other types of paprika can be substituted, but the flavor of the broth will be decidedly different. Serves 4

{ Although often overlooked by home cooks, mussels and other shellfish need only very short cooking in a flavorful broth to produce a delicious main course. Here, they are the centerpiece of a leisurely Spanish-style dinner, with each course served separately. A loaf of crusty bread is perfect for soaking up the broth, while a zesty red wine, such as Rioja or tempranillo, will marry well with the food.

⅓ cup olive oil
3 garlic cloves, thinly sliced
1 teaspoon pimentón (Spanish smoked paprika)
¼ teaspoon crushed red-pepper flakes
1 cup dry white wine
⅓ cup bottled clam juice
1 pound mussels, debearded and cleaned (see page 260)
2 pounds clams, preferably cockles, cleaned (see page 260)
4 plum tomatoes, seeded and diced (scant 2 cups)
¼ cup loosely packed chopped fresh flat-leaf parsley leaves
3 tablespoons unsalted butter, cut into pieces
Coarse salt and freshly ground pepper

Heat oil in a large pot over medium. Cook garlic, stirring, until softened and lightly browned, about 1 minute. Stir in pimentón and red-pepper flakes, then pour in wine and clam juice. Raise heat to medium-high, and bring to a boil.

Add mussels and clams to the pot. Cover and steam 3 minutes, then stir in the tomatoes. Cover and cook 3 minutes more (discard any shellfish that do not open). Turn off heat, and stir in parsley and butter until combined and heated through. Season with salt and pepper. Serve immediately, ladling shellfish and broth into shallow bowls.

Roasted Parsnip and Chorizo Bites

Try serving these tapas-style appetizers at a cocktail party, with other passed hors d'oeuvres. Makes 8

    1   to 2 parsnips
    2   teaspoons olive oil
        Coarse salt and freshly ground pepper
    8   slices (each cut diagonally ¼ inch thick) spicy chorizo
        (1 to 2 ounces)
    1   ounce Manchego cheese

Preheat oven to 425°F. Peel parsnips and cut into ¼-inch-thick slices on the diagonal (you should have at least 16 pieces). Toss slices with the oil, and season with salt and pepper. Spread in a single layer on a rimmed baking sheet; roast until lightly browned, 12 to 13 minutes, flipping the slices halfway through.

Remove from oven. Push parsnips to one side of pan and add chorizo; roast just to heat chorizo through, about 2 minutes. Let cool 5 minutes.

Meanwhile, break cheese into ½-inch chunks. While still warm, layer half the parsnip slices with chorizo and a piece of cheese, then top with remaining parsnip slices. Spear each stack with a toothpick, and serve warm.

Orange and Endive Salad

The key to this salad is the quality of each of the ingredients. Navel oranges are seedless and very juicy, but any type of orange can be used (just remove seeds from slices, if necessary). And choose a high-quality, fruity olive oil (preferably a Spanish variety). Serves 4

    3   oranges, preferably navel
    2   small heads endive, trimmed and cut lengthwise into
        long strips
    ⅓   cup loosely packed mint leaves, torn if large
    1   cup loosely packed flat-leaf parsley leaves, torn if
        large
    2   tablespoons good-quality extra-virgin olive oil, plus
        more for drizzling
        Coarse salt and freshly ground black pepper
        Pinch of cayenne pepper

Using a sharp knife, slice off both ends of each orange, then slice to remove peel and bitter white pith, following the curve of the fruit. Cut each orange crosswise into five rounds.

Toss the endive, mint, and parsley with the oil, and season with salt and black pepper. Arrange oranges on a platter; sprinkle with cayenne and season with salt and black pepper. Scatter endive mixture over oranges. Just before serving, drizzle lightly with more oil.

A vibrant citrus salad makes a refreshing palate cleanser, bridging savory and sweet. A last-minute splash of flavorful olive oil brings it all together.

Choosing Chocolate

Dark chocolate, including semisweet and bittersweet, imparts a deep, rich flavor and color to baked goods and other desserts. Choose chocolate with a high percentage (at least 61%) of cacao, the ingredient responsible for chocolate's distinctive taste. The darkest chocolate, sometimes called baking chocolate, is made entirely of cacao. Other dark chocolates contain sugar and sometimes vanilla in varying proportions; milk is added to produce milk chocolate. Choose the best-quality chocolate you can find; Valrhona, Callebaut, Scharffen Berger, and El Rey are all top-quality brands. Store chocolate, tightly wrapped, in a cool, dry place. A serrated knife is the best tool for chopping chocolate finely or coarsely, as directed.

Dark Chocolate Puddings

For the best flavor, use bittersweet chocolate with at least 61 percent cacao. Serves 4

For pudding
- ¼   cup packed light-brown sugar
- 2   tablespoons cornstarch
- 2   tablespoons unsweetened Dutch-process cocoa powder
- ¼   teaspoon salt
- 1   cup milk
- 1   cup heavy cream
- 2   large egg yolks
- 4   ounces bittersweet chocolate, coarsely chopped (about 1 cup)
- ½   teaspoon pure vanilla extract

For whipped cream
- ½   cup heavy cream
- ¼   teaspoon ground cinnamon
- 2   tablespoons confectioners' sugar
     Pinch of salt

Make pudding: Prepare an ice-water bath. Whisk together brown sugar, cornstarch, cocoa powder, and salt in a 4-quart saucepan to combine. Add milk, cream, and yolks; whisk over medium-high heat until mixture comes to a boil and thickens, 3 to 4 minutes. Remove from heat. Whisk in the chocolate and vanilla, whisking until chocolate has melted and mixture is smooth. Strain through a fine sieve into a heatproof bowl. Set bowl in the ice bath, and stir gently until cool.

Divide evenly among four 6-ounce ramekins or custard cups. Cover with waxed paper or plastic wrap, pressing it directly on the surface of each pudding to prevent a skin from forming. Refrigerate at least 30 minutes (or up to 2 days).

When ready to serve, prepare the whipped cream: Whisk all ingredients together in a chilled bowl until medium peaks form. Spoon a generous dollop on each pudding.

{ Made with
brown sugar,
cocoa powder,
and bittersweet
chocolate, these
puddings have
an incomparable
taste and luxuri-
ously creamy
consistency. The
topping has a hint
of cinnamon.

A farmhouse hard cider, such as one from Normandy, France, has a balance of fruitiness and effervescence that pairs deliciously with the rich, sweet, and tangy flavors in this hearty meal. Beer, of course, is equally appropriate for the casual mood; try a Belgian ale or Weissbeer. If you prefer wine, an off-dry riesling would be especially at home.

Pork Chops with Sautéed Apples and Onion
Shaved Fennel-Celery Salad
Mustard Mashed Potatoes
Maple Custards

PREPARATION SCHEDULE

1. Bake custards; chill.

2. Make slaw; let rest at least 30 minutes.

3. Cook pork chops; cover to keep warm. Meanwhile, boil potatoes.

4. Sauté apples and onion.

5. Mash potatoes, and serve.

Pork Chops with Sautéed Apples and Onion

In this updated take on pork chops and applesauce, apple wedges are cooked with onion and then chicken stock until soft but still holding their shape; the cooking liquid becomes thick and saucy. Serves 4

- 4   bone-in pork chops (each 8 to 9 ounces and 1 inch thick)
     Coarse salt and freshly ground pepper
- 2   tablespoons safflower or other neutral-tasting oil
- 1   yellow onion, thinly sliced
- 3   apples, such as Honeycrisp, Fuji, or Gala, cored and cut into ¼-inch wedges
- 2   tablespoons brandy
- 1½ cups chicken stock, homemade (see page 260) or low-sodium store-bought
- 2   tablespoons unsalted butter, room temperature

Preheat oven to 400°F. Pat dry pork with paper towels, and season both sides with salt and pepper. Heat oil in a large skillet over medium-high until hot but not smoking. Cook chops until golden brown on the bottom, 2 to 3 minutes. Turn with tongs; cook until brown on other side, about 1 minute. Transfer chops to a baking sheet. Roast until an instant-read thermometer inserted in thickest part (avoiding bone) reaches 138°F, about 8 minutes. Remove from oven; tent with parchment paper, then foil, to keep warm.

Return skillet to medium-high heat. Cook onion until translucent, stirring occasionally, about 3 minutes. Add apples; cook, stirring frequently, until beginning to soften, about 5 minutes. Pour in brandy; heat until evaporated, scraping up browned bits from bottom of pan with a wooden spoon.

Add stock and bring to a boil. Reduce heat and simmer, partially covered, until liquid has thickened to a sauce, about 15 minutes. Stir in butter, season with salt and pepper. To serve, arrange pork chops on top of the apple mixture on a platter.

Mustard Mashed Potatoes

To give the dish a more rustic appeal, the potatoes are left unpeeled and are coarsely mashed after cooking. Serves 4

- 1½ pounds small Yukon Gold potatoes (unpeeled)
     Coarse salt
- 2   tablespoons whole-grain mustard
- ¼   cup plus 1 tablespoon extra-virgin olive oil
- ¼   cup plus 2 tablespoons chicken stock, homemade (see page 260) or low-sodium store-bought
- 2   tablespoons coarsely chopped fresh flat-leaf parsley

Place potatoes in a 4-quart saucepan; cover with water by 2 inches and add salt. Bring to a boil over high heat, then reduce heat and simmer until potatoes are tender when pierced with the tip of a sharp knife, about 22 minutes.

Drain potatoes in a colander and return to hot pot for 2 minutes to dry out, shaking pan occasionally. Mash with a potato masher; add mustard, oil, stock, and parsley. Blend with masher to combine; season with salt. Serve warm.

Shaved Fennel-Celery Salad

A mandoline, including a Japanese model such as Benriner, makes easy work of slicing the vegetables paper-thin, but you could use a very sharp chef's knife instead. Kohlrabi is available in pale-green and red varieties; green kohlrabi, which looks a bit like white turnips, is used here to make a white and green slaw. Serves 4

- 1 fennel bulb, trimmed, cored, and sliced paper-thin crosswise
- 1 head kohlrabi, peeled (with a sharp paring knife) and sliced paper-thin
- 2 celery stalks, sliced diagonally (about 1 cup)
- 3 tablespoons apple cider vinegar
- 1 tablespoon Dijon mustard
- 1 tablespoon honey
- ¼ cup walnut oil
  Coarse salt and freshly ground pepper

Toss together fennel, kohlrabi, and celery in a large bowl. In a small bowl, whisk together vinegar, mustard, honey, and oil until combined; season with salt and pepper.

Pour vinegar mixture over the fennel mixture and toss to coat evenly. Cover tightly and let sit at room temperature for at least 30 minutes (or up to 1 hour) before serving.

Maple Custards

Be sure to buy only pure maple syrup; robust grade B is often the best choice for cooking and baking. Makes 4

- ¼ cup plus 1 tablespoon pure maple syrup, plus more for serving (optional)
- 5 large egg yolks
- ½ teaspoon pure vanilla extract
- 1 cup heavy cream
- ½ cup whole milk

Preheat oven to 350°F. Whisk together maple syrup, yolks, and vanilla in a heatproof bowl. Heat cream and milk in a small saucepan over medium until just beginning to bubble, about 3 minutes. Very slowly pour hot-cream mixture over maple-syrup mixture (to prevent curdling), stirring constantly with a wooden spoon, until combined.

Divide evenly among four 6- or 8-ounce ramekins or custard cups; place in a baking dish. Fill dish with enough hot water to come three-quarters up sides of ramekins.

Bake until custards are just set in the center, 35 to 40 minutes. Use tongs to remove custards from the hot water, then chill in the refrigerator until ready to serve, at least 10 minutes (or up to overnight, covered with plastic wrap). Serve cold or at room temperature. If desired, drizzle more maple syrup over the custards before serving.

An aged rum or brandy would play off the caramel sweetness of the maple syrup in these custards (and serve as a great after-dinner digestif).

Braised chicken and soft polenta combine to make a comforting cool-weather dish; the vintage rimmed yellowware plates are just deep enough to contain the pan sauce. A generous-size baked dip that goes straight from the oven to the table, served with crusty bread, starts off the meal on a convivial note.

Warm Swiss Chard and Bacon Dip
Braised Chicken Marsala
Sage Polenta
Sautéed Pears in Honey Syrup

PREPARATION SCHEDULE

1. Brown chicken and transfer to oven.
2. Cook polenta; prepare dip and spread in baking dish.
3. Remove chicken from oven; raise oven temperature.
4. Bake dip, and serve; finish sauce for chicken.
5. Sauté pears just before serving.

Braised Chicken Marsala

Serves 4

- 4   skin-on, bone-in chicken thighs (about 1¼ pounds)
- 4   chicken drumsticks (about 1 pound)
  Coarse salt and freshly ground pepper
- 1   tablespoon extra-virgin olive oil
- 2   red onions, peeled and quartered through the stem
- 2   plum tomatoes, cut into 1-inch pieces
- 6   sprigs thyme
- ¾   cup Marsala (sweet Italian fortified wine)
- 1¼ cups chicken stock, homemade (see page 260) or low-sodium store-bought
  Sage Polenta

Preheat oven to 400°F. Rinse chicken, pat dry with paper towels, and season both sides with salt and pepper. Heat oil in a large, high-sided sauté pan over medium-high. Working in batches, brown chicken on both sides, turning once, 10 to 12 minutes. Transfer chicken to a platter; tent loosely with parchment paper, then foil, to keep warm. After all chicken is browned, pour off excess fat.

Add onions, tomatoes, and thyme to the pan. Cook, stirring occasionally, until golden brown, about 4 minutes. Pour in Marsala; cook until reduced by half, about 5 minutes. Return chicken to pan and pour in stock; bring to a simmer. Transfer to oven; cook until chicken is cooked through and tender, about 35 minutes. Transfer chicken to a platter, and cover to keep warm.

Skim off excess fat from liquid in pan; simmer liquid over medium-high until slightly thickened, about 5 minutes. To serve, divide polenta among shallow bowls and arrange chicken on top; spoon pan sauce over each.

Sage Polenta

If the polenta is ready before the rest of the meal, keep it in the pan and press parchment or waxed paper directly on the surface to prevent a skin from forming; partially covering the pan with the lid will also work. Stir well before serving. Serves 4

- 5   cups water, plus more as needed
  Coarse salt and freshly ground pepper
- 1   cup coarse Italian polenta
- 2   tablespoons finely chopped fresh sage
- 3   tablespoons unsalted butter, room temperature

Bring the water to a boil in a large saucepan over high heat, then add 2 teaspoons salt. Whisking constantly, add polenta in a slow, steady stream and return to a boil. Reduce heat to a very low simmer. Cover partially; cook, stirring occasionally, until mixture is creamy and starting to pull away from the sides of the pan, about 40 minutes, adding sage in last 5 minutes. If polenta is too thick to stir, add more water (up to ½ cup), a little at a time, and continue cooking, stirring occasionally.

Remove from heat. Stir in butter, and season with pepper and more salt, as desired. Serve hot.

Warm Swiss Chard and Bacon Dip

Serves 4

1   tablespoon olive oil
3   strips bacon (3 ounces), cut crosswise into
    ½-inch pieces
½   yellow onion, cut into small dice (about ¾ cup)
2   tablespoons all-purpose flour
⅓   cup heavy cream
½   cup milk
8   ounces Swiss chard, large stems removed, leaves cut
    crosswise (8 cups)
    Coarse salt and freshly ground pepper
¼   cup freshly grated Parmesan cheese
    Toasted bread, for dipping

Preheat oven to 450°F. Heat oil in a sauté pan over medium
until hot but not smoking. Cook bacon, stirring frequently,
until golden, 5 to 6 minutes. Add onion and cook, stirring
occasionally, until translucent, about 3 minutes. Sprinkle in
the flour. Cook, stirring constantly, until light golden, about
3 minutes. Whisk in cream and milk; continue whisking
until mixture has thickened, 1 to 2 minutes. Add chard; cook
until wilted, 5 minutes. Season with salt and pepper.

Spread chard mixture in a shallow 1-quart baking dish;
sprinkle with cheese. Bake until bubbling and golden on
top, about 15 minutes. Serve hot, with toasted bread.

Sautéed Pears in Honey Syrup

*Juniper berries provide distinctive flavor to the dish, but you
can omit them, if you prefer. Serves 4*

2   tablespoons unsalted butter
3   ripe but firm Bosc pears, quartered and cored
6   juniper berries, crushed with the side of a large knife
    and coarsely chopped (optional)
½   cup mild honey, such as clover
1½ tablespoons fresh lemon juice

Melt butter in a large skillet over medium-high heat. Add
pear wedges, cut sides down, and juniper berries (if using);
cook until pears are golden, about 6 minutes. Turn pears
onto other cut sides, and cook 1 minute.

Pour in honey, gently swirling skillet to coat pears evenly,
and reduce heat to medium-low. Cook until pears are
softened and glazed, about 3 minutes. Pour lemon juice
over pears and stir syrup to combine.

To serve, divide pears among four dessert plates and spoon
syrup over the top.

A substantial meal like this calls for a light dessert. If you like, you can wait until after dinner has been served to begin cooking the pears; they take just 10 minutes from start to finish.

Sweet and delicate bay scallops have a brief season each fall in the Northeast (when they are also available in specialty fish markets nearly everywhere). Served as a midweek supper or a weekend lunch, this meal is a nice way to showcase their flavor—and take advantage of their quick-cooking nature.

Green Salad with Apple Dressing
Bay Scallops with Lemon Butter and Herbs
Celery Root and Potato Puree
Jam-Glazed Hazelnut Mini Cakes

PREPARATION SCHEDULE

1. Roast beets for salad; raise oven temperature.

2. Bake cakes, and let cool.

3. Meanwhile, boil celery root and potatoes; drain and puree.

4. Whisk together apple mixture for salad. Make jam glaze, and let cool (drizzle over cakes just before serving).

5. Sauté scallops, and assemble salad.

Bay Scallops with Lemon Butter and Herbs

Make sure the skillet (do not use nonstick) is very hot before adding the oil. Heat the oil sufficiently before adding the scallops so that they sear to a crust quickly. Also, wait to salt them until after cooking; otherwise, the salt will draw out the moisture and prevent a crust from forming. Serves 4

- 1 pound bay scallops (about 50), tough muscles removed
- 2 tablespoons safflower or other neutral-tasting oil
  Coarse salt and freshly ground pepper
- 2 tablespoons unsalted butter
- ¼ cup fresh lemon juice (from 2 lemons)
- ½ cup assorted fresh herbs, such as chives, flat-leaf parsley, dill, and chervil, snipped into ½-inch pieces
  Lemon wedges, for serving
  Celery Root and Potato Puree

Pat dry scallops with paper towels. Heat a large skillet over high until very hot. Add oil, tilting to coat the pan. When oil is hot but not smoking, add scallops in a single layer without crowding. Reduce heat to medium-high; cook, without stirring, until golden brown on the bottom, 1 to 2 minutes, then toss and cook 1 minute more, or until scallops are opaque throughout. Season with salt and pepper.

Transfer scallops to a plate and tent with parchment paper, then foil, to keep warm. Add butter to skillet; when melted, pour in lemon juice and swirl to combine.

Divide puree evenly among shallow bowls. Top with scallops; spoon pan sauce on top and sprinkle with herbs. Serve with lemon wedges.

Celery Root and Potato Puree

Celery root, or celeriac, can be intimidating because of its gnarled surface, but once you trim away the fibrous peel it resembles a white turnip, with a mild earthy flavor. Although potatoes typically turn gluey when pureed in a food processor, the celery root keeps them from doing so here. Serves 4

- 1¼ pounds (about 2 small) celery root, peeled and cut into 2-inch pieces
- ½ pound Yukon Gold potatoes (about 1 medium), peeled and cut into 2-inch pieces
- 2 garlic cloves (peeled)
  Coarse salt and freshly ground pepper
- 2 tablespoons unsalted butter
- ¼ cup milk

Combine celery root and potato in a 4-quart saucepan, and cover with water by about 2 inches. Add garlic and salt. Bring to a boil, then reduce heat to a simmer; cook (uncovered) until vegetables are tender when pierced with a fork, about 20 minutes. Drain in a colander and return to hot pot to dry out for 5 minutes, shaking pot occasionally.

While still hot, puree celery root, potatoes, and garlic in a food processor just until smooth (do not overprocess); transfer to a warmed serving bowl.

Melt butter in a small saucepan over medium heat. Add milk and heat until hot but not yet bubbling; pour over puree, and stir just to combine. Season with salt and pepper, and serve.

Green Salad with Apple Dressing

The beets can be roasted and peeled a day ahead; let cool, then refrigerate in an airtight container. Serves 4

    1   pound small or medium beets, trimmed, rinsed
    ¼   cup extra-virgin olive oil
        Coarse salt and freshly ground pepper
    1   shallot, minced (2 to 3 tablespoons)
    1   tablespoon white wine vinegar
    ½   Granny Smith apple, cut into ¼-inch dice (1 cup)
    4   cups loosely packed baby romaine, green leaf, or
        other tender salad greens (about 5 ounces)

Preheat oven to 375°F. Place beets in a baking dish. Toss with 1 tablespoon oil; season with salt. Pour ¼ cup water into pan. Cover dish with parchment, then foil; bake until beets are tender when pierced with the tip of a sharp knife, 45 to 55 minutes. When cool enough to handle, peel off skin. Cut beets into ¾-inch-thick wedges.

In a bowl, whisk shallot with vinegar and apple; season with salt and pepper. Slowly pour in remaining 3 tablespoons oil, whisking until combined.

To serve, toss greens with some of the apple mixture and divide among plates. Toss beets in the remaining apple mixture, and spoon over greens.

Jam-Glazed Hazelnut Mini Cakes

If you can't find blanched hazelnuts, peel them yourself; see page 260 for the instructions. Makes about 1½ dozen

    5   tablespoons unsalted butter, plus more for tins
    ½   cup all-purpose flour, plus more for tins
    ½   cup whole blanched hazelnuts (1½ ounces), finely
        ground (⅓ cup)
    ½   cup sugar
    ½   teaspoon salt
    3   large egg whites
    1   tablespoon brandy
    ½   cup seedless raspberry jam
    2   to 3 teaspoons water

Preheat oven to 400°F. Brush 18 cups of mini muffin tins with butter, and dust lightly with flour; tap out excess. Melt the butter in a medium skillet over medium-high heat. When it begins to sizzle, reduce heat to medium. Cook, swirling skillet occasionally, until butter is lightly browned. Skim foam from top, leaving liquid butter behind; remove from heat and let cool.

Whisk together flour, ground hazelnuts, sugar, and salt in a medium bowl. Add egg whites, and whisk until smooth. Stir in brandy. Pour in cooled butter, leaving any dark brown sediment in skillet; whisk to combine. Let stand 20 minutes at room temperature.

Ladle 1 tablespoon batter into each prepared cup, filling each about two-thirds full. Bake, rotating tins halfway through, until a toothpick inserted in centers comes out clean, about 13 minutes. Transfer to a wire rack to cool 10 minutes before turning out cakes. (Cakes can be cooled completely and kept overnight at room temperature in an airtight container.)

Heat jam and 2 teaspoons water in a small saucepan over medium, stirring, until melted. (The glaze should be thick but still pourable from a spoon; if necessary, thin with 1 teaspoon more water.) Remove from heat, and let cool to room temperature. Drizzle a spoonful over each cake just before serving.

Ground hazel-
nuts, brandy, and
browned butter
flavor these tiny
cakes; the rasp-
berry glaze pro-
vides an easy and
colorful flourish.
Serve with Darjeel-
ing or your favorite
variety of hot tea.

winter

Many home cooks welcome winter with glee, since it affords much occasion to spend time in the kitchen and to host family and friends. So what if the weather outside is frightful? All the more reason to start cooking. And what could be better for warming the senses than to prepare, and then enjoy, a cold-weather meal of roast chicken breasts in creamy tarragon sauce, glazed endive, and poached pears with chocolate sauce? It doesn't require hours of cooking, either. Hearty après-ski appetites will find satisfaction in cheese fondue followed by crisp pork cutlets and egg noodles. Winter also means holidays, and you'll find festive menus here for small-scale gatherings, including spice-rubbed beef filets accompanied by glazed pearl onions and potato puree and topped off with chocolate truffles. Chicken liver mousse on toast points and beef broth with carrots, leeks, and almost-from-scratch mushroom dumplings (using store-bought wonton wrappers) are good ways to ring in the new year. Any day is a good day for an update on classic steak frites, here made with hanger steak and oven-baked shoestring fries. With soulful menus like these, you're sure to savor the season.

winter menus

Invite friends over for a casual-sounding meal of soup, sandwiches, and salad, then surprise them with a trio of dishes that are out of the ordinary (yet still simple to prepare). Oysters are an elegant addition to a rich, velvety soup, served in a bowl whose shape brings to mind an oyster shell.

Creamy Oyster Soup
Crisp Ham and Cheese Sandwiches
Celery Root and Walnut Salad
Pear and Dried Cherry Baked Custard

PREPARATION SCHEDULE

1. Make salad; refrigerate.

2. Soak cherries; assemble sandwiches.

3. Mix and bake custard.

4. Cook sandwiches; keep warm.

5. Make soup, and serve.

Creamy Oyster Soup

This recipe calls for shucked oysters and their "liquor," which can be found in tubs or tins at fish markets and is a crucial component of the soup. Serves 4

- 2   tablespoons unsalted butter
- 1   large shallot, minced (about ¼ cup)
- 2   large celery stalks, finely chopped (about ½ cup)
- 3   tablespoons all-purpose flour
- 2   tablespoons dry vermouth or sherry
- ½   cup heavy cream
- 4   cups milk
      Coarse salt and freshly ground pepper
- ¾   pound shucked oysters with liquor (about 1½ cups)
      Paprika, for sprinkling

Melt butter in a 4-quart saucepan over medium heat. Add shallot and celery; cook, stirring occasionally, just until beginning to turn translucent, about 3 minutes. Add flour, and cook, stirring, until light golden, about 1 minute.

Stir in vermouth, then add cream, whisking constantly; cook, whisking, until thickened and smooth, about 2 minutes. Slowly whisk in milk, and season with salt and pepper, whisking well to combine. Simmer, stirring occasionally, until thickened, about 3 minutes.

Reduce heat to medium-low. Add oysters and their liquor; cook, stirring occasionally, just until edges of oysters begin to curl, about 2 minutes. Season with salt and pepper. Ladle soup evenly into four bowls, and sprinkle with paprika; serve immediately.

Both the salad and the sandwiches can rest a bit before being served, so you can enjoy the soup, clear the table, and proceed without any further tending-to. The sandwiches will still be warm and melting with cheese, the celery salad cool and crisp.

Crisp Ham and Cheese Sandwiches

Speck is a cured and smoked ham with a salty-sweet flavor; prosciutto, which is cured but not smoked, can be used instead. Ciabatta loaves are best for making pressed sandwiches; look for the mini loaves at specialty bakeries or food shops (or cut larger ciabatta loaves into six-inch lengths). If you have a panini press, use it in place of the pans suggested here. Makes 4

- 4   mini ciabatta loaves, halved lengthwise
- 8   thin slices provolone cheese (about 6 ounces)
- 8   thin slices Black Forest ham (about 2 ounces)
- 8   thin slices speck or prosciutto (about 2 ounces)
- 1   cup loosely packed baby spinach leaves
      Coarse salt and freshly ground pepper
- 3   tablespoons unsalted butter, room temperature

Top each of 4 ciabatta halves with 1 slice of provolone, 2 slices of Black Forest ham, 2 slices of speck, ¼ cup spinach leaves, and 1 more slice of provolone. Season with salt and pepper, and top with the other bread halves. Spread tops and bottoms of sandwiches evenly with the butter.

Heat a large cast-iron skillet over medium-low. Place 2 sandwiches in pan; weight with another heavy pan. Cook until first side is golden, about 2 minutes. Flip sandwiches, press with weight, and cook until other side is golden, about 2 minutes. Transfer sandwiches to a platter; cover with parchment paper, then foil, and place in a warm spot (such as near the oven). Wipe skillet with a paper towel; repeat to cook remaining 2 sandwiches. Serve warm.

Celery Root and Walnut Salad

A mandoline makes easy work of slicing the celery root thinly and evenly, but a sharp chef's knife will also do. Serves 4

- 1   tablespoon plus 1 teaspoon Dijon mustard
- 2   tablespoons red wine vinegar
- ¾   cup walnuts
      Coarse salt and freshly ground pepper
- 1   pound celery root, peeled, thinly sliced, and cut into matchsticks
- 1   cup loosely packed fresh flat-leaf parsley leaves

Stir together mustard, vinegar, and walnuts in a bowl; season with salt and pepper. Add celery root and parsley, and toss to coat. Cover with plastic wrap; refrigerate until ready to serve, at least 20 minutes (and up to 1 hour).

Pear and Dried Cherry Baked Custard

The batter for this fruit-filled custard (a French dessert known as clafouti) comes together quickly in a blender. Serves 4

-      Unsalted butter, for baking dish
- ¼   cup all-purpose flour, plus more for dusting
- ½   cup dried cherries
- 1   ripe pear, preferably D'Anjou, peeled, halved lengthwise, and cored
- ¾   cup milk
- ¾   cup heavy cream
- 2   large eggs
- 1   teaspoon pure vanilla extract
- ¼   cup sugar
      Pinch of salt

Preheat oven to 400°F. Butter a 10-inch fluted tart dish or pie plate. Dust with flour; tap out excess. Put cherries in a bowl; cover with boiling water by 1 inch. Let stand until plump, about 10 minutes.

Cut pear lengthwise into ⅛-inch-thick slices; fan slices in bottom of prepared dish. Process remaining ingredients in a blender until smooth, about 1 minute. Pour batter over pear slices. Drain cherries; sprinkle over batter. Bake until golden and set, about 25 minutes. Let stand at least 15 minutes before cutting into wedges.

Tart Apple Bistro Salad
Hanger Steak with Caramelized Shallots
Oven-Baked Shoestring Fries
Caramel Pudding

PREPARATION SCHEDULE

1. Make custard, and refrigerate.

2. Marinate steak; caramelize shallots.

3. Cook steak.

4. Meanwhile, cut potatoes into matchsticks, and bake.

5. While steak rests, make vinaigrette and assemble salad.

Hanger Steak with Caramelized Shallots

Hanger steak is very flavorful and tender, so be sure not to overcook (medium at most), and slice against the grain for the best texture. Serves 4

- ½ cup extra-virgin olive oil
- ¼ cup sherry vinegar
- 2 garlic cloves, crushed with the side of a large knife
- 1 tablespoon plus 1 teaspoon Dijon mustard, plus more for serving
- 1 tablespoon Worcestershire sauce
- 1½ pounds hanger steak (about 10 inches long and 1¼ inches thick)
- 5 shallots, peeled and halved or quartered
  Coarse salt and freshly ground pepper
- ¼ cup water

{ In this version of the French bistro classic known as *steak frites*, hanger steak gets marinated in a mustard-garlic blend. Shallots are caramelized in the same pan, and shoestring potatoes are baked, rather than fried. Serve the steak with more mustard on the side and a luscious red wine, such as Burgundy or Côtes du Rhône.

Whisk together ¼ cup oil, the vinegar, garlic, mustard, and Worcestershire sauce in a large glass dish. Place steak in dish, and turn to coat with marinade. Let marinate at room temperature 20 minutes, turning once halfway through.

Meanwhile, heat 2 tablespoons oil in a large skillet over medium-high. Cook shallots, stirring often, until just golden, 2 to 3 minutes. Reduce heat to medium-low. Season shallots with salt and continue cooking, adding the water 2 tablespoons at a time as needed to keep shallots from sticking, until tender and caramelized, 15 to 18 minutes. Transfer shallots to a plate.

Wipe skillet with paper towels. Heat remaining 2 tablespoons oil over medium-high. Remove steak from marinade, letting excess drip back into dish (discard marinade). Pat dry steaks with paper towels, then season both sides with salt and pepper. Cook steak, turning once, until an instant-read thermometer registers 135°F for medium-rare, 8 to 9 minutes per side. Transfer to a platter. Let rest 10 minutes, tenting with parchment paper, then foil, to keep warm. Season with pepper.

Wipe skillet again; return shallots to pan and quickly toss over medium heat. Thinly slice steak across the grain. Serve with shallots and mustard.

{ Hanger steak is seared to a delightful crust while remaining tender and juicy inside. The caramelized shallots are returned to the skillet after the steak has been cooked, then tossed with the juices.

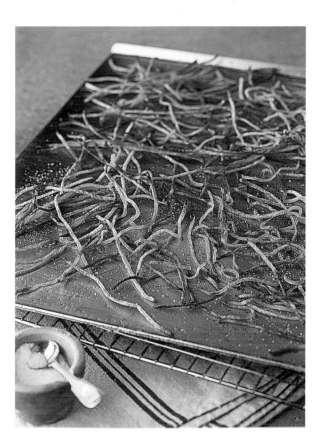

Tart Apple Bistro Salad

Featuring the bright taste of herbs and the tartness of apple, this salad is a refreshing starter for the heartier dishes that follow. It can also be served after the steak, as a sort of palate cleanser before dessert. Serves 4

- ¼ cup extra-virgin olive oil
- 1½ teaspoons champagne vinegar
- ¾ teaspoon Dijon mustard
- 1 teaspoon honey
  Coarse salt
- 1 small head romaine lettuce, cut or torn into small pieces
- 1 small head frisée, separated into small pieces
- ½ tart green apple, such as Granny Smith, cored and thinly sliced
- ¼ cup loosely packed fresh flat-leaf parsley leaves
- 6 fresh chives, snipped into ¾-inch pieces (about 3 tablespoons)

Whisk together oil, vinegar, mustard, and honey in a large bowl; season with salt. Add romaine, frisée, apple, parsley, and chives, and toss to coat. Serve immediately.

Oven-Baked Shoestring Fries

Using a mandoline to cut the potatoes into ultra-thin shapes (or "shoestrings") is quick and easy. You can do so up to four hours ahead; to prevent discoloration, place cut potatoes in a bowl of cold water in the refrigerator until ready to use, then gently pat dry with paper towels. Serves 4

- 3 tablespoons olive oil, plus more for baking sheets
- 2 russet potatoes (about 1½ pounds), peeled and cut into shoestrings
  Coarse salt and freshly ground pepper

Preheat oven to 425°F. Lightly coat two baking sheets with oil. Toss together potatoes, oil, and 1 teaspoon salt in a bowl. Dividing evenly among prepared baking sheets, arrange potatoes in a single layer.

Bake, turning potatoes with a metal spatula a few times and rotating sheets halfway through, until crisp and golden brown, 18 to 20 minutes. Transfer potatoes to a large piece of parchment paper; let cool 5 minutes, then season with salt and pepper, and serve.

Caramel Pudding

In this version of crème caramel, the dessert is not baked; instead, a small amount of gelatin is used as a thickener. The caramel sauce can be refrigerated in a covered container for up to one week; bring to room temperature before using. The custard can be refrigerated, covered with plastic wrap, for up to one day. Serves 4

  1 teaspoon unflavored gelatin
  ½ cup plus 2 tablespoons water, plus 2 teaspoons
       for gelatin
  1 cup sugar
  2 large eggs plus 1 egg yolk
  1 cup heavy cream
  ½ cup milk
       Pinch of salt

Stir gelatin and 2 teaspoons water in a small bowl until dissolved.

Cook ¾ cup sugar in a large skillet over medium-high heat, without stirring, until sugar at edges begins to melt and turn clear, about 3 minutes. Continue to cook, stirring constantly with a wooden spoon, until medium amber in color, 1½ to 2 minutes. Remove from heat. Carefully stir in remaining ½ cup plus 2 tablespoons water. (If sugar begins to solidify, return pan to medium heat until melted.) Let caramel cool completely.

Prepare an ice-water bath. Whisk whole eggs and the yolk in a medium bowl. Bring cream, milk, remaining ¼ cup sugar, and the salt to a simmer in a medium saucepan over medium-high heat. Whisk half the hot cream mixture into the eggs. Pour this mixture back into saucepan. Add gelatin mixture; whisk until combined. Reduce heat to low. Cook, stirring constantly, just until mixture is thick enough to coat the back of the spoon, about 3 minutes.

Pour custard into a heatproof bowl set in the ice bath. Let cool completely, stirring constantly, about 3 minutes. Transfer to a shallow serving bowl. Refrigerate until set, at least 30 minutes. Pour caramel over custard. To serve, spoon into cups or bowls.

How to Make Caramel

If you've never attempted it before, you may be surprised to find that making caramel from scratch is quite easy. One traditional technique calls for cooking the sugar and water together without stirring, and occasionally washing down the sides of the pan with a damp pastry brush to prevent sugar crystals from forming. For the method used here, the sugar is simply melted and stirred until it reaches the right color, then water is carefully added at the end. You do need to keep a careful eye on the pan to avoid overcooking, as color is the best indicator of doneness. Depending on the specific recipe, the caramel should be a medium amber hue, not too light or too dark; dip a strip of white paper into the bubbling liquid to accurately gauge the color.

The combination of rich custard and sweet caramel is hard to resist, but not to prepare. To fit the relaxed mood, the dessert is chilled in a large bowl—instead of in individual portions—and then spooned into teacups at the table.

Each component of this artfully arranged Japanese-style dinner requires only about five ingredients (including pantry staples) and minimal preparation: The fish is broiled, the sweet potatoes are roasted (and accompanied by a citrus-soy sauce for dipping), and the spinach is wilted, then combined with a sesame-seed dressing and patted into log shapes. Serve with glasses of well-chilled sake.

Broiled Red Snapper
Citrus-Soy Sweet Potatoes
Sesame-Spinach Rolls
Rice Pudding with Candied Kumquats

PREPARATION SCHEDULE

1. Cook rice pudding; simmer kumquats, and let cool completely.

2. Meanwhile, roast sweet potatoes and mix sauce for dipping.

3. Wilt spinach, chop, then toss with dressing; form into logs.

4. Broil snapper, and serve.

5. Top pudding with kumquats just before serving.

Broiled Red Snapper

This dish relies on the broiler to brown the skin to a delectable crisp; rotate the pan as necessary to ensure even cooking. This method would also work well for striped bass. Serves 4

1 tablespoon safflower or other neutral-tasting oil
4 small red snapper fillets (6 ounces each)
Coarse salt and freshly ground pepper
½ English cucumber, peeled and cut into 2-inch-long matchsticks
1 pint (3 ounces) radish sprouts or alfalfa sprouts (or thinly sliced radishes)

Heat broiler, with rack 4 inches from heat source. Coat a baking sheet with the oil. Use a paper towel to blot excess moisture from fish. With a sharp knife, make two or three small slits in the skin side of each fillet, then season both sides with salt and pepper. Place on prepared baking sheet, skin sides up.

Broil, rotating sheet for even browning, until skins are crisp and flesh is opaque throughout, 6 to 8 minutes. Remove from oven. Arrange fish on a serving platter, and top with cucumber and sprouts.

Sesame-Spinach Rolls

This spinach dish—inspired by a Japanese favorite called oshi toshi—can be enjoyed hot, cold, or at room temperature. To chill, form rolls while spinach is still warm, then let cool completely before refrigerating up to one day in an airtight container. A mortar and pestle is a good way to grind the sesame seeds, but a spice grinder or clean coffee grinder can be used instead. Serves 4

2 tablespoons sesame seeds, toasted (see page 260) and coarsely ground
1 tablespoon plus 1 teaspoon sake (Japanese rice wine)
1 teaspoon soy sauce, preferably tamari
1 teaspoon rice wine vinegar (unseasoned)
¼ cup water
1 pound spinach, tough stems discarded, washed well and dried

Mix the ground sesame seeds, sake, soy sauce, and vinegar in a small bowl.

Heat the water in a large skillet over medium-high until simmering. Add spinach; cover and steam 2 minutes, then toss with tongs and continue cooking (covered) 2 minutes more. Toss again to thoroughly wilt, and transfer spinach to a colander; press with a wooden spoon or flexible spatula to extract as much liquid as possible.

Coarsely chop spinach, and place in a bowl. Add sesame dressing, tossing to combine well. Divide evenly into four portions, and shape each into a compact log.

Citrus-Soy Sweet Potatoes

Here the sweet potatoes are cut into rounds so they contrast with the shape of the other dishes, but any cut will do (try spears made by halving crosswise, then quartering lengthwise); just be sure the pieces are similar in size for even cooking. Serves 4

- 3 sweet potatoes, scrubbed and cut crosswise into 1-inch rounds
- 1 tablespoon safflower or other neutral-tasting oil
  Coarse salt
- ¼ cup soy sauce, preferably tamari
- ¼ cup fresh lemon juice (from 2 lemons)
- 3 tablespoons water

Preheat oven to 400°F. On a large rimmed baking sheet, toss sweet potatoes with the oil; season with salt. Spread in a single layer; roast, flipping slices halfway through, until tender and lightly browned, about 25 minutes.

Meanwhile, mix soy sauce, lemon juice, and the water in a small bowl.

Serve sweet potatoes with sauce on the side for dipping.

Rice Pudding with Candied Kumquats

Kumquats, among the smallest members of the citrus family, have tart flesh inside a sweet, edible skin. Choose ones that are slightly firm, with no soft spots. Look for sushi rice at Asian markets and specialty food stores. Serves 4

For pudding
- 1½ cups water
- ⅔ cup sushi rice
- 3½ cups milk
- ¼ cup plus 1 tablespoon sugar
- ¼ teaspoon salt

For candied kumquats
- ½ pound kumquats, sliced into ¼-inch-thick rounds, seeds removed
- ½ cup water
- ¾ cup sugar

Make pudding: Combine the water, rice, milk, sugar, and salt in a small heavy-bottommed saucepan; bring to a boil over medium-high heat. Reduce heat to a simmer; cook (uncovered), stirring often to prevent rice from sticking to bottom of pan, until mixture is thickened (but there is still some liquid remaining) and rice is soft, 18 to 20 minutes.

Meanwhile, make candied kumquats: Combine kumquats with the water and sugar in a small saucepan, and bring to a boil over medium-high heat. Reduce to a simmer; cook, stirring occasionally, until the fruit skins are tender and translucent and liquid is syrupy, about 25 minutes. Remove pan from heat; let kumquats cool completely in liquid.

Pour rice pudding into a 9-by-13-inch dish, and cover with parchment, waxed paper, or plastic wrap, pressing it directly on surface of pudding. Refrigerate 45 to 60 minutes. To serve, divide pudding evenly among dessert bowls, and spoon candied kumquats over each.

Sushi rice is used to make this sweet pudding. With a steaming pot of herbal tea, it's the perfect ending for the meal. Colorful candied kumquats (and charming wooden spoons) are served alongside; the fruits are simmered in simple syrup to tame their tartness.

Cheese Fondue
Crisp Pork Cutlets
Egg Noodles with Sautéed Brussels-Sprouts Leaves
Cherry Compote over Chocolate Ice Cream

PREPARATION SCHEDULE	1. Mix sour cream sauce for pork; bread cutlets.	2. Boil noodles; prepare cherry compote.	3. Make fondue, and serve.	4. Sauté Brussels sprouts, and finish dish; fry pork cutlets.	5. Assemble dessert just before serving.

Crisp Pork Cutlets

If cutlets vary in thickness, use a meat mallet to pound the pork between two pieces of plastic wrap to make even (about one-quarter inch). Serves 4

- ½ cup sour cream
- ½ teaspoon caraway seeds, crushed with the side of a large knife
- ½ teaspoon spicy brown mustard
  Coarse salt and freshly ground pepper
- 3 large eggs
- 1 cup all-purpose flour
- 3 cups panko (Japanese bread crumbs)
- 8 pork cutlets (about 1 pound total)
- 1 cup safflower or other neutral-tasting oil

Mix sour cream with caraway seeds and mustard, and season with a pinch each of salt and pepper.

Whisk the eggs in a shallow dish. Season the flour with 1 teaspoon salt and ½ teaspoon pepper; spread on a plate. Put the panko in a resealable plastic bag and crush slightly with a rolling pin; place on another plate.

Season pork on both sides with salt and pepper. Dredge cutlets in flour mixture, turning to coat both sides, then dip in the eggs, letting excess drip back into dish. Place in panko, pressing crumbs into the pork to coat entirely.

Heat the oil in a large sauté pan over medium until hot but not smoking. Working in two batches, cook until pork is golden brown and crisp on the first side, about 2 minutes; turn pork and cook until golden brown on the other side, about 2 minutes more. Transfer to paper towels and blot dry, then place on a platter. Season with salt and pepper.

Egg Noodles with Sautéed Brussels-Sprouts Leaves

Serves 4

- 1 pound Brussels sprouts
  Coarse salt and freshly ground pepper
- 8 ounces egg noodles
- 2 tablespoons extra-virgin olive oil, plus more for drizzling
- 1 garlic clove, minced
- 4 tablespoons (½ stick) unsalted butter, cut into pieces
- 2 tablespoons capers, drained and rinsed
- ¼ cup coarsely chopped fresh flat-leaf parsley
  Finely grated zest of 1 lemon (about 2 tablespoons), plus 1 tablespoon juice

Halve Brussels sprouts through the stem. Trim away core and pull leaves apart. Bring a large pot of water to a boil; add salt. Boil noodles according to package instructions. Reserve ⅓ cup cooking water. Drain noodles; drizzle with oil.

Heat oil in a large sauté pan over medium. Cook garlic until softened, stirring, 2 minutes. Add Brussels-sprouts leaves, tossing to coat, and reserved cooking water. Cook over medium-high, tossing, until leaves are tender, 5 minutes. Add noodles and butter; cook, tossing, until warmed through. Transfer to a bowl. Add remaining ingredients; toss to combine. Season with salt and pepper.

{ Breaded and pan-fried cutlets are a staple of quick cooking everywhere. Here, they are paired with egg noodles tossed with tender Brussels-sprouts leaves and a tangy caraway cream sauce. A cheese fondue and the cherry-chocolate dessert round out this meal in Swiss-chalet fashion.

A ceramic fondue pot and wood-handled spears are the most authentic tools for making and serving this nostalgic dish; a candle keeps the melted cheese warm and at the right consistency for dipping. Pour what remains of the wine used to flavor the fondue at the table.

Cheese Fondue

Two varieties of cheese make for a rounded, complex fondue. Appenzeller cheese, a classic choice, has a pronounced aroma and tangy taste; Gruyère is a good substitute. Gouda provides a subtle, nutty flavor reminiscent of caramel; other mild cows'-milk cheese, such as Prima Donna or Edam, can be used instead. Kirsch, a clear cherry brandy, is optional, but highly recommended because it adds a hint of fruitiness to the fondue and also helps offset the richness. Serves 4

- 4   ounces aged Gouda (preferably up to 3 years)
- 2   ounces Appenzeller cheese
- 1   tablespoon all-purpose flour
    Pinch of freshly ground white pepper
    Pinch of cayenne pepper
- ¾   cup dry or off-dry riesling wine or gewürztraminer
- 1   teaspoon Kirsch (optional)
- ½   loaf (1 pound) dense rustic bread, crust removed, cut into 1-inch cubes
- 1   cup drained cornichons
- ½   cup drained cocktail onions

Cut both types of cheese into small (½-inch) cubes; toss in a bowl with the flour, white pepper, and cayenne to coat. Bring the wine to a simmer in a fondue pot (or a small saucepan) over medium-low heat. Add cheese, and reduce heat to medium-low; cook, whisking, until cheese is melted and mixture is smooth, about 5 minutes.

Add Kirsch (if using); continue cooking, stirring, until combined. Remove from heat. Set fondue pot over a warming candle (or transfer contents to a warm serving dish). Serve immediately with the bread, cornichons, and onions.

Cherry Compote over Chocolate Ice Cream

Using frozen cherries allows you to make a quick and delicious fruit compote out of season—plus, there's no pitting required. Serves 4

- 1   package (10 ounces) frozen cherries
- ¼   cup sugar
- 1   tablespoon fresh lemon juice
- 2   tablespoons brandy
- 1   pint best-quality chocolate ice cream
- 1   bar (3.5 ounces) good-quality bittersweet chocolate, cut into chunks

Bring cherries and sugar to a simmer in a small saucepan over medium heat; cook until the sugar has dissolved and the mixture has reduced slightly, about 3 minutes.

Remove from heat. Stir in lemon juice and brandy to combine; let cool.

To serve, scoop ice cream into four bowls; spoon compote over the top, and sprinkle with chocolate chunks.

Artichokes on Toast
Spaghetti with Clams
Wilted Chicory Salad
Grapefruit in Moscato

PREPARATION SCHEDULE

1. Boil water for pasta; make bruschetta.
2. Partially cook spaghetti, and drain. Cook clams.
3. Make salad.
4. Finish cooking spaghetti with sauce.
5. Make dessert just before serving.

Spaghetti with Clams

In this interpretation of pasta con vongole (with clams), a classic Italian dish, spaghetti replaces the typical linguine (which could well be substituted). Serves 4

Coarse salt and freshly ground pepper
1   pound spaghetti
2   tablespoons extra-virgin olive oil
2   garlic cloves, minced (about 1½ teaspoons)
1   small dried chile pepper, crumbled, or a pinch of crushed red-pepper flakes
1½ pounds littleneck clams, cleaned (see page 260)
1   cup dry white wine
2   tablespoons coarsely chopped fresh flat-leaf parsley, plus whole leaves for garnish
Juice of 1 lemon (about 3 tablespoons)
3   tablespoons unsalted butter

Bring a large pot of water to a boil; add 1 tablespoon salt. Cook spaghetti 2 minutes less than package instructions. Drain pasta, reserving 1 cup cooking water.

Meanwhile, heat oil in a large skillet over medium. Cook garlic and chile pepper, stirring frequently, until garlic is golden, about 2 minutes. Add clams and wine. Bring to a boil over high heat; cover, and cook, shaking pan occasionally, until clams open, 3 to 4 minutes (discard any that do not open). Stir in chopped parsley. Transfer to a bowl.

Return skillet to medium-high. Bring reserved pasta water and lemon juice to a simmer; cook until slightly reduced, about 3 minutes. Remove from heat; whisk in butter. Add clams and spaghetti. Cook over medium-low heat until pasta is al dente, 2 to 3 minutes. Season with salt and pepper; garnish with parsley leaves.

Wilted Chicory Salad

This is a quick and delicious side dish for any season, as chicory is available year-round. Radicchio, a red-leaf relative of chicory, adds contrasting color. You can certainly make the salad without the anchovies, but it won't be anywhere near as flavorful. Serves 4

2   tablespoons extra-virgin olive oil
2   anchovy fillets, coarsely chopped (optional)
1   head radicchio (about 10 ounces), trimmed and sliced into ½-inch pieces
1   bunch chicory (about 1½ pounds), trimmed and roughly chopped
Coarse salt and freshly ground pepper
Balsamic vinegar, for drizzling

Heat oil in a large skillet over medium-high. Add anchovies, and cook 1 minute. Add radicchio and chicory; sauté until slightly wilted, 1 to 2 minutes. Season with salt and pepper. Transfer to serving bowl and drizzle with balsamic vinegar. Serve immediately.

{ Tender strands of spaghetti in a chile-spiked clam sauce form the heart of a rustic supper that makes the best of a winter pantry. Jarred artichoke hearts and fresh ricotta top toasted bread for an appetizer, and anchovies and balsamic vinegar punch up a warm chicory salad that follows the pasta.

Artichokes on Toast

Frozen artichoke hearts may be used in place of jarred. You will need to thaw them slightly before sautéing with the garlic, as well as increase the cooking time by three to four minutes to ensure proper browning. Serves 4

- 2 garlic cloves (peeled)
- 4 slices (about ¾ inch thick) rustic bread
- 1 tablespoon extra-virgin olive oil, plus more for drizzling
- 1 jar (12 ounces) marinated artichoke hearts, drained
- ½ cup fresh ricotta cheese
   Coarse salt and freshly ground pepper
   Shaved Parmigiano-Reggiano cheese, for garnish

Preheat oven to 375°F. Thinly slice 1 garlic clove; halve the other one. Toast bread slices on a baking sheet for about 8 minutes, turning halfway through. Rub halved garlic clove over toasted slices. Place on a serving platter.

Heat oil in a medium skillet over medium-high. Sauté sliced garlic and artichoke hearts until golden, stirring occasionally, 3 to 4 minutes.

Season ricotta with salt and pepper; spread about 2 tablespoons on each slice of bread. Top with sautéed garlic and artichokes. Season with salt and pepper. Garnish with shaved cheese; drizzle with olive oil.

Grapefruit in Moscato

Moscato d'Asti, a sweet sparkling Italian wine, makes a fine match for the slightly bitter grapefruit in this dessert. You can substitute a drier sparkling wine or even Champagne for different—but still delicious—results. Serves 4

- 1 ruby red grapefruit, chilled
- 4 sugar cubes, preferably turbinado or demerara (raw)
- 1 bottle (750-ml) Moscato d'Asti

Cut top end off grapefruit, and remove peel and bitter white pith with a sharp paring knife. Carefully carve out segments from between membranes. Place 1 sugar cube and several grapefruit segments in each serving glass, and fill with Moscato. Serve immediately.

This invigorating dessert (or after-dinner cocktail—take your pick) is like a ray of sunshine on a wintry day. The effervescence of the sparkling wine helps to dissolve the sugar quickly and to refresh the palate.

Hoisin-Glazed Hens
Spicy Cucumber-Scallion Pickles
Citrus-Cashew Salad
Kiwi Fruit in Jasmine Tea Syrup

PREPARATION SCHEDULE

1. Rub, stuff, and tie hens; refrigerate.

2. Steep tea and make syrup; refrigerate.

3. Roast hens; pickle cucumbers and scallions.

4. Meanwhile, cook rice, if serving; toss salad.

5. Slice kiwis and assemble dessert just before serving.

Hoisin-Glazed Hens

Hoisin—a thick, dark blend of soybeans, garlic, chiles, and spices—is available in the Asian section of most supermarkets; the flavor can vary greatly, so choose a high-quality brand, such as Kikkoman or Lee Kum Kee. Serves 4

- 4 Cornish hens (2 pounds each), rinsed and patted dry
- 3 garlic cloves, minced
- 2 tablespoons minced peeled fresh ginger (from a 2-inch piece)
- 2 fresh red chiles, ribs and seeds removed, minced (about 2 tablespoons)
- 1 bunch cilantro, sprigs separated
- ½ cup hoisin sauce, plus more for basting

Preheat oven to 400°F. Place hens in a large roasting pan. Mix garlic, ginger, and chiles in a small bowl; rub mixture over hens and under skin, and stuff cavities with cilantro sprigs, dividing evenly. Tie legs of each hen together with kitchen twine. Cover pan; refrigerate 20 minutes.

Remove hens from refrigerator, and brush with the hoisin sauce, dividing evenly. Roast, basting occasionally with extra sauce, until an instant-read thermometer inserted into the thigh (avoiding bone) registers 170°F, 45 to 50 minutes. Remove from oven, and serve hot.

Spicy Cucumber-Scallion Pickles

These pickled green vegetables pack a bit of heat— and a lot of crunch. Serve them with or without white rice. Serves 4

- ½ English cucumber, peeled and cut into 2-inch-long strips
- 4 scallions, trimmed and cut into 2-inch pieces
- 1 cup rice wine vinegar (unseasoned)
- ¼ cup sugar
- ½ teaspoon salt
- ¼ teaspoon crushed red-pepper flakes
- 4 cups cooked white rice, for serving (optional)

Toss together cucumber and scallions in a nonreactive shallow bowl.

Combine vinegar, sugar, salt, and red-pepper flakes in a small saucepan over medium heat. Cook, stirring, until the sugar and salt have dissolved, 2 to 3 minutes. Pour over the cucumber and scallions, and let stand 30 to 40 minutes (but no longer, or the texture will not be as crisp).

To serve, use a slotted spoon to transfer vegetables from pickling liquid to four plates, dividing evenly; serve over rice, if desired.

{ It's only slightly more work to prepare four small hens than a whole chicken, and the outcome—a gorgeously glazed hen on each plate—is worth it. The rest of the meal can be prepared while the hens "marinate" in the fridge, then roast in the oven.

Citrus-Cashew Salad

If clementines are unavailable, mandarin oranges and pixie tangerines make excellent substitutes. Serves 4

- 2   clementines
- 6   kumquats
- 4   celery stalks
- ½   cup whole roasted salted cashews, some broken into large pieces
- 1   tablespoon plus 1 teaspoon fresh lemon juice
- 1   tablespoon plus 1 teaspoon extra-virgin olive oil
- 2   teaspoons honey
     Freshly ground pepper

Peel clementines and separate fruit into segments; place segments in a bowl. Slice kumquats into very thin rounds, and remove seeds. Add rounds to bowl.

Using a mandoline or very sharp knife, thinly slice celery diagonally. Add to bowl with fruit along with cashews, and toss to combine.

Whisk together lemon juice, oil, and honey; season with pepper. Drizzle over citrus mixture in bowl; toss to combine. Divide among four small bowls, and serve.

Kiwi Fruit in Jasmine Tea Syrup

The finest jasmine green tea comes in "pearls," which are hand-rolled and have a pronounced fragrance; look for them at tea shops and specialty stores. It is important not to steep the tea for too long, or it will turn bitter. To peel the kiwis, slice off both ends with a knife, then carefully slide a spoon between the flesh and skin, working your way around the fruit. Scoop out the flesh in one piece. Serves 4

- 1   tablespoon loose-leaf jasmine green tea
- ½   cup boiling water
- ½   cup sugar
- 4   kiwi fruit, peeled and sliced into ½-inch rounds

Place tea in a heatproof cup. Pour ¼ cup boiling water over tea and let steep 5 minutes; strain through a fine sieve, discarding solids.

Bring sugar and remaining ¼ cup water to a boil in a small saucepan, stirring occasionally to dissolve sugar. Reduce heat, and simmer 5 minutes. Remove from heat, and stir in the brewed tea. Let cool completely, then refrigerate, covered, until ready to use, up to 1 day.

Divide sliced kiwis among four bowls, and drizzle with cooled syrup.

Kiwi fruit is often used as a component in winter mixed-fruit salads, but here it is the star attraction for dessert; a simple syrup steeped with jasmine tea is drizzled over the top.

Inspired by Nordic flavors, this relaxed meal evokes fireside dining, as do the campsite-style dishes and wood-handled flatware.
A creamy cauliflower gratin is hearty enough to serve as a main
course; its richness is balanced by the bitterness of radicchio in a
salad layered with seasonal cranberries and crisped chestnuts.

Apples and Smoked Trout on Rye Crisps
Cauliflower Gratin
Radicchio and Chestnut Salad
Coffee with Cognac and Cardamom

PREPARATION SCHEDULE

1. Make cardamom syrup.

2. Bake gratin; assemble trout appetizers, and serve.

3. Whip cream for coffee drink; refrigerate.

4. Toss salad, and serve with gratin.

5. Make coffee drinks after dinner.

Cauliflower Gratin

Panko provides a crunchy texture to the top of this gratin. Look for it at Asian markets, specially food stores, and supermarkets. Serves 4

4 tablespoons (½ stick) unsalted butter, plus more for baking dish
2 shallots, thinly sliced (½ cup)
   Coarse salt and freshly ground pepper
¼ cup all-purpose flour
2 cups milk
¼ teaspoon freshly grated nutmeg
2 teaspoons Dijon mustard
1¼ cups grated Gruyère cheese
1 head cauliflower (1¾ pounds), stalks trimmed, florets cut into 2- to 3-inch pieces (about 6 cups)
¼ cup panko (Japanese bread crumbs)

Preheat oven to 375°F. Melt 3 tablespoons butter in a saucepan over medium heat. Cook shallots with a pinch of salt, stirring occasionally, until shallots are golden, 5 to 6 minutes.

Sprinkle flour into pan and stir with a wooden spoon until smooth; cook, stirring, 1 minute (it should not take on any color). Whisking constantly, gradually add milk until incorporated, then add nutmeg and 1 teaspoon salt. Cook until liquid is bubbling around edges of pan, then reduce heat; cook at a bare simmer until thickened, stirring frequently and scraping bottom of pan to prevent lumps from forming, 4 to 5 minutes. Add mustard and 1 cup cheese, stirring to combine, then season with pepper.

Meanwhile, generously butter a 2-quart baking dish. Bring a pot of water to a boil; add salt. Cook cauliflower until

just tender when pierced with the tip of a sharp knife, 4 to 5 minutes. Drain well and transfer to prepared dish.

Pour cheese sauce over cauliflower, stirring gently to coat. Sprinkle with panko and remaining cheese, then dot with remaining tablespoon butter. Bake until bubbling and golden, 35 to 40 minutes. Let cool slightly before serving.

{ This no-cook starter is a study in contrasts, with the flavors of tart apple, creamy mustard sauce, smoky trout, and earthy whole-grain crisps in every bite. For authenticity, serve the starters with chilled Aquavit, a Scandinavian spirit flavored with caraway and other herbs.

Apple and Smoked Trout on Rye Crisps

Serves 4

- ½ cup crème fraîche
- ¼ cup Dijon mustard
- 8 rye or whole-grain crispbread crackers, such as Finn Crisps or Wasa Crisps
- ½ tart green apple, such as Granny Smith
- 2 smoked trout fillets (4 to 6 ounces), broken into 1-inch chunks
  Freshly ground pepper

Stir together crème fraîche and mustard in a small bowl. Spread some sauce on each crispbread. Cut apple lengthwise into two wedges (remove core); slice very thinly into half moons. Dividing evenly, top crispbread with apple, then trout. Sprinkle with pepper, and drizzle with any remaining sauce. Serve immediately.

Radicchio and Chestnut Salad

Treviso, a type of radicchio, has a more elongated shape than the more familiar supermarket variety, which can be used instead. Other chicories, such as escarole and curly endive, would also work well. Chestnuts that have been peeled and packed in jars or bottles can be found at most supermarkets, especially during the holiday season. Serves 4

- ¼ cup dried cranberries
- 3 tablespoons plus 1 teaspoon balsamic vinegar
- ¼ cup extra-virgin olive oil
- 1 jar (7 ounces) peeled whole chestnuts, halved lengthwise
- ¼ red onion, thinly sliced
- 1 large head treviso or other radicchio, halved and cut lengthwise into thin strips (6 cups)
  Coarse salt and freshly ground pepper

Combine cranberries and vinegar in a bowl; let stand 10 minutes. Heat 3 tablespoons oil in a medium skillet over medium. Cook chestnuts in a single layer until lightly browned and beginning to turn crisp, tossing occasionally, about 5 minutes. Remove pan from heat; use a slotted spoon to transfer chestnuts to a plate.

Add cranberries and vinegar to skillet, stirring while vinegar reduces, 1 minute. Stir in remaining tablespoon oil. Place radicchio and onion in a large bowl. Pour in warm cranberry mixture; sprinkle with chestnuts. Season with salt and pepper, and toss to combine.

Coffee with Cognac and Cardamom

This drink is similar to Irish coffee, with brandy standing in for whiskey. Cardamom-laced simple syrup is the only sweetener you'll need. For best results, use strong coffee. Serves 4

- ⅔ cup water
- ⅔ cup sugar, preferably turbinado (raw) or demerara
- 6 whole cardamom pods, lightly crushed with the side of a large knife
- 1½ cups heavy cream
- ⅔ cup Cognac or other brandy
- 2 cups plus 2 tablespoons freshly brewed coffee

In a 4-quart saucepan over medium heat, bring the water and sugar to a simmer, stirring to dissolve sugar; turn off heat. Add cardamom; let steep 20 minutes.

Meanwhile, whip cream to soft peaks with an electric mixer; refrigerate, covered, until ready to serve.

Pour brandy and hot coffee into a pitcher; strain cardamom syrup mixture into pitcher, and stir to combine. To serve, divide among four glasses and top each with a generous dollop of whipped cream.

Roast Chicken Breasts in Creamy Tarragon Sauce
Warm Lentils with Spinach
Caramelized Endive
Poached Pears with Chocolate Sauce

PREPARATION SCHEDULE

1. Poach pears; make chocolate sauce.

2. Cook lentils; rub chicken with tarragon-butter, and roast.

3. Roast endive (on a lower rack); toss lentils with spinach.

4. Remove chicken from oven; make pan sauce.

5. Assemble desserts just before serving.

Roast Chicken Breasts in Creamy Tarragon Sauce

Rubbing the herbed butter under and over the skins will ensure that the lean breast meat becomes moist and flavorful as it cooks. Serves 4

4   skin-on, bone-in chicken breast halves (about 12 ounces each)
4   tablespoons (½ stick) unsalted butter, room temperature
2   tablespoons snipped fresh chives
3   tablespoons finely chopped fresh tarragon, plus 10 whole leaves
    Coarse salt and freshly ground pepper
½   cup heavy cream
¼   cup chicken stock, homemade (see page 260) or low-sodium store-bought

Preheat oven to 450°F, with rack in upper level. Rinse chicken, and pat dry with paper towels. In a small bowl, mix butter, chives, chopped tarragon, and ½ teaspoon each salt and pepper. Rub butter mixture over chicken and under skin (use your fingers to gently lift skin and spread butter underneath as evenly as possible). Season chicken all over with salt, then place in a roasting pan. Roast, rotating pan halfway through, until skin is crisp, about 25 minutes.

Mix cream, stock, and whole tarragon leaves. Remove pan from oven; tilt pan to allow juices to pool on one side, then spoon out and discard almost all of the juices. Pour cream mixture into pan; use a large spoon to baste chicken with it. Return to oven; cook until cream mixture is bubbling and slightly thickened, 5 to 7 minutes.

Transfer chicken breasts to four plates. Whisk cream mixture in hot pan, incorporating browned bits from bottom of pan; spoon a little sauce over chicken, then pour remaining sauce into a small pitcher or gravy boat to serve on the side.

{ French classics made easy: Roasting only the chicken breasts, rather than the whole bird, cuts the cooking time in half (and there's no need for carving); a creamy sauce is cooked in the same pan. Endive shares oven time with the chicken, becoming sweet and caramelized; lentils require brief cooking and no soaking. Waffle-weave tea towels serve as informal placemats.

Roasting Vegetables

Roasting is one of the easiest and best ways to prepare vegetables—especially in the long winter months. The oven's high heat condenses the vegetables' natural sugars, creating a lovely brown color and a delicate balance of savory and sweet flavors. You can roast just about any vegetable by coating it lightly in olive or other flavorful cooking oil, sprinkling with coarse salt and freshly ground pepper (and herbs and spices, as desired), and cooking in a hot oven (between 350°F and 450°F). Drizzling with a bit of vinegar, as in the recipe for the endive, results in a nice glaze; it also adds a bit of sharpness. Small vegetables, such as new potatoes and baby carrots, can be roasted whole, but most often you will want to cut them into smaller portions. This also exposes more of the surface for caramelization. Be sure to toss the vegetables a few times while roasting to encourage even browning.

Caramelized Endive

If you want to substitute other vegetables for the roasted endive in this menu, try shallots or fennel. Serves 4

- 4 heads Belgian endive, halved lengthwise
- 2 tablespoons extra-virgin olive oil
    Coarse salt and freshly ground pepper
- 2 tablespoons sherry vinegar

Preheat oven to 450°F. Place endive on a large rimmed baking sheet; drizzle with the oil, and season with salt and pepper, turning endive to coat evenly. Cook, cut sides down, until browned and caramelized on the bottom, 15 to 18 minutes.

Remove from oven. Drizzle endive with vinegar, shaking pan to coat evenly. Return to oven and cook until nicely glazed, 5 to 7 minutes. Serve hot or warm.

Warm Lentils with Spinach

French green lentils, often called lentils du Puy, are smaller and hold their shape better than brown lentils. Look for them at specialty food shops, natural-food stores, and many super-markets. Serves 4

- 1 cup French green lentils
- 2 celery stalks, finely chopped
- 2 shallots, minced
- 2 garlic cloves, minced
- 2 tablespoons extra-virgin olive oil
- 3 cups loosely packed baby spinach leaves
    (about 4 ounces)
    Coarse salt and freshly ground pepper

Combine lentils, celery, shallots, and garlic in a 4-quart saucepan, and cover with water by 2 inches. Bring to a boil over medium-high heat. Reduce heat to medium-low; stir once or twice, then simmer, partially covered, until lentils are tender but not falling apart, 25 to 30 minutes. Drain, and discard cooking liquid.

Transfer lentil mixture to a bowl; add oil, stirring to combine. Add spinach, and toss until slightly wilted. Season generously with salt (about 1 teaspoon) and pepper.

Endive is most familiar as a salad and in hors d'oeuvres, but its delicate, slightly bitter flavor can be enhanced by cooking. Here it is roasted in the oven until caramelized, then drizzled with vinegar and returned to the oven briefly just until nicely glazed.

Poaching Pears

Choose pears that are firm (they should give only slightly at both ends), with stems attached; avoid those with blemishes or soft spots. Most supermarket pears have spent a few months in cool storage, so they are usually still a few days away from being fully ripe. You can speed the ripening process by placing the fruit in a brown paper bag with an apple or a banana; the pears will soon be ready to eat. If you plan on poaching or cooking the fruit, make sure it is a bit underripe so it'll hold its shape.

Poached Pears with Chocolate Sauce

Small and especially sweet-tasting, Forelle pears are good candidates for poaching; Seckel pears, which are similar in size, can be used instead, or try other sweet, juicy varieties, such as Comice and Bartlett (choose the smallest ones you can find, or else cook a few minutes longer to ensure they become tender). Riesling, available in dry and off-dry (slightly sweet) varieties, is a good choice for poaching pears. Serves 4

- 4   small ripe but firm pears, preferably Forelle
- 4   cups water
- ¾   cup dry or off-dry white wine, such as riesling
- ⅓   cup packed light-brown sugar
- 1   vanilla bean, split lengthwise, seeds scraped and reserved
- 6   ounces bittersweet chocolate, preferably at least 61% cacao, coarsely chopped
     Waffle cookies and whipped cream, for serving (optional)

Peel the pears, then core them from the bottom, using a small melon baller to scoop out the seeds while keeping the pears intact. Cut a round of parchment paper to fit inside a 4-quart saucepan. Place pears in pan along with the water, wine, brown sugar, and vanilla bean and seeds. Bring to a boil over medium-high heat, then reduce to a simmer. Cover pears with the parchment round; poach, gently turning pears occasionally to coat with liquid, until very tender (they should be easily pierced with the tip of a sharp knife) but not falling apart, 10 to 15 minutes, depending on ripeness and size. Use a slotted spoon to transfer pears to a bowl; cover with the parchment round. Remove vanilla bean (discard).

Place chopped chocolate in a heatproof bowl. Return saucepan to high heat, and boil poaching liquid until reduced to a thin syrup consistency, about 10 minutes. Pour 1 cup syrup over the chocolate, and stir to melt. Cover chocolate sauce and set in a warm spot (such as near the stove) until ready to use. If the chocolate sauce becomes too thick to pour, reheat it over a pot of simmering water (or melt very briefly in the microwave). Pour remaining syrup over pears and refrigerate, covered with parchment, until cool.

To serve, place a pear in each of four dessert bowls, and drizzle with chocolate sauce; if desired, rest a cookie in each bowl, and dollop whipped cream on the side.

Pears and chocolate make an unbeatable combination. Here
the fruit is poached until tender enough to eat with a spoon.
The vanilla-infused cooking liquid is then reduced and mixed
with bittersweet chocolate for a luscious sauce. The hem-
stitched napkins are the same buttery shade as the fruit; silver
chargers look festive beneath clear octagonal dessert bowls.

Potpie may seem like a lot of work, but using ready-made puff pastry shortens the preparation time (there's no need to mix and chill your own dough) and guarantees a flaky crust. These individual vegetarian pies are hearty enough to please all appetites. The baking dishes—actually vintage pudding molds—and serving tray are ironstone.

Butter Lettuce with Brie and Pears
Curried Vegetable Potpies
Spiced Lemon Cookies

PREPARATION SCHEDULE

1. Mix dough, and bake cookies; raise oven temperature.

2. Cut pastry dough into squares, and refrigerate.

3. Cook potpie filling; assemble potpies, and bake.

4. Toss cooled cookies in sugar.

5. Assemble salad, and serve.

Curried Vegetable Potpies

Some curry mixes are stronger than others, so adjust the amount used according to your taste preference. You will need four ten-ounce baking dishes, such as ramekins or individual pie plates. Serves 4

- 1 package (17.3 ounces) frozen puff pastry dough, thawed according to package instructions
- 3 tablespoons unsalted butter
- 1 leek, white and pale green parts only, cut into ½-inch half-moons, washed well (see page 260)
- 3 parsnips, peeled and cut into 1-inch pieces
- 2 carrots, peeled and cut into 1-inch pieces
   Coarse salt and freshly ground pepper
- 3 tablespoons all-purpose flour
- 4 cups milk, plus more for brushing
- 1 russet potato (about 8 ounces), peeled and cut into 2-by-½-inch matchsticks
- 1 tablespoon plus 1 teaspoon curry powder
- 1 cup frozen peas (unthawed)

Preheat oven to 400°F. Cut pastry dough into four squares (each about 4 inches, just larger than an inverted baking dish). Make several slits in the dough for steam vents. Chill squares on a baking sheet until firm, 15 to 30 minutes.

Meanwhile, melt butter in a 4-quart saucepan over medium-high. Cook leek, parsnips, and carrots with 1 teaspoon salt, stirring frequently, until slightly soft, 3 to 5 minutes. Add flour; cook, stirring, until golden, 1 to 2 minutes.

Whisking constantly, stir in milk, potato, and curry powder. Bring to a boil; reduce heat, and simmer very gently until potato is tender, stirring occasionally, 8 to 10 minutes. Season with salt and pepper.

Divide cooked vegetable mixture evenly among baking dishes. Stir ¼ cup peas into each dish, then top with a square of puff pastry. Brush pastry lightly with milk. Place on a baking sheet and bake until crust is golden and filling is bubbling, 22 to 25 minutes. Let cool 10 minutes before serving.

Butter Lettuce with Brie and Pears

Fruit and cheese go hand in hand; here pears and Brie combine in a wintry salad to follow the potpies. Marcona almonds—a sweet, buttery variety from Spain, often sautéed or roasted in olive oil and salt—add crunch to the mix. You can use regular almonds instead. Serves 4

2   heads butter or Boston lettuce, leaves separated
8   slices (¼ inch thick) Brie (8 ounces), softened
1   ripe but firm pear, preferably D'Anjou, cored and cut into ¼-inch-thick slices
½   cup Marcona almonds (about 2 ounces)
2   tablespoons fresh lemon juice
1   teaspoon Dijon mustard
2   teaspoons honey, preferably orange blossom
2   tablespoons good-quality extra-virgin olive oil
    Coarse salt and freshly ground pepper

Tear lettuce into 2-inch pieces. Arrange 2 slices of Brie on each of four plates. Divide pear slices evenly among plates, fanning them next to cheese. Mound lettuce on top, and scatter almonds around plate.

Whisk together lemon juice, mustard, honey, and oil; season with salt and a generous grinding of pepper. Drizzle evenly over pear and lettuce; serve immediately.

Spiced Lemon Cookies

Using a mortar and pestle is a great way to crush the coriander seeds, but you can also place them on a cutting board and crush them with the side of a large knife. Makes 1 dozen

1½   teaspoons coriander seeds, coarsely crushed
1   cup plus 2 tablespoons all-purpose flour
¼   teaspoon salt
½   cup (1 stick) unsalted butter, room temperature
½   cup confectioners' sugar, plus more for tossing
    Finely grated zest of 1 lemon (about 2 tablespoons)

Preheat oven to 350°F. Whisk together crushed coriander, flour, and salt.

With an electric mixer on medium-high speed, cream butter until pale and fluffy. Add the confectioners' sugar, and beat until smooth. Add flour mixture and lemon zest; mix just to combine.

Pinch off dough by the tablespoon and roll each into a ball. Space 2 inches apart on a parchment-lined baking sheet. Bake, rotating sheet halfway through, until cookies are lightly golden around edges, about 20 minutes. Transfer cookies to a wire rack to cool completely. (Cooled cookies can be kept up to 1 week at room temperature in an airtight container.) Before serving, toss cookies in confectioners' sugar to coat, tapping off excess sugar.

Cookies like these are a good option for dessert—even on busy weeknights. The dough can be quickly prepared, formed into balls, and baked—no rolling or chilling required. The cooled cookies are tossed in confectioners' sugar before serving. Honey-sweetened hot tea (Earl Grey and Darjeeling are especially nice) complements their delicate lemon-and-coriander flavor; here it is served in English creamware cups.

Duck Breast with Fig Sauce
Braised Red Cabbage
Grated Potato Cake
Hazelnut Brittle over Ice Cream

PREPARATION SCHEDULE

1. Make brittle. Score duck, and season; let rest.

2. Meanwhile, braise cabbage and fry potato cake.

3. Sear duck, then transfer to oven.

4. While duck rests, make fig sauce; bake potato cake.

5. Assemble dessert just before serving.

Duck Breast with Fig Sauce

Duck breasts are available at butcher shops and specialty food shops, as well as many supermarkets. They render quite a lot of fat as they cook. If you like, strain the fat and refrigerate up to a month; use it for roasting or frying potatoes or making duck confit. Serves 4

- 2 duck breasts (1 pound each)
  Coarse salt and freshly ground pepper
- 1 tablespoon olive oil
- 1 large shallot, thinly sliced
- ⅓ cup dry sherry
- ⅓ cup fig jam
- ½ cup chicken stock, homemade (see page 260) or low-sodium store-bought
- 2 teaspoons unsalted butter
- 1 teaspoon fresh lemon juice

Preheat oven to 400°F. Using the tip of a sharp knife, score the duck breasts at ¼-inch intervals in a crosshatch pattern, cutting deeply into the fat but not the meat. Season duck all over with 1 teaspoon salt and a generous pinch of pepper. Let stand at room temperature 20 to 30 minutes.

Heat oil in a 10-inch cast-iron skillet over medium-low until hot but not smoking. Add duck breasts, skin sides down; cook until browned and crisp, about 5 minutes. Turn breasts, and transfer to oven; roast until an instant-read thermometer inserted in thickest part (avoiding bone) registers 130°F for medium-rare, 10 to 12 minutes. Remove pan from oven, and transfer duck to a cutting board; let rest.

Meanwhile, pour off rendered duck fat into a heatproof container. Return 2 tablespoons duck fat to the pan (reserve the rest for another use, or discard). Add shallot; cook over medium heat until beginning to brown, stirring occasionally, about 2 minutes. Carefully add the sherry (it will spatter), and cook 1 minute, then stir in fig jam and cook 1 minute more. Pour in stock; cook, stirring, until sauce is thick and emulsified. Add butter; cook, stirring, until combined, 1 minute. Remove from heat; stir in lemon juice.

To serve, thinly slice duck diagonally against the grain; divide among four plates. Spoon fig sauce over duck.

Duck breast has many qualities that make it appealing to the home cook: It is naturally flavorful (thanks to a generous layer of fat that is rendered during cooking), simple to prepare, and always impressive. Earthy red cabbage and shredded-potato cakes lend down-to-earth flavors to the otherwise elegant meal. The subtly patterned plates are creamware.

Grated Potato Cake

If you don't have any cheesecloth, use a clean kitchen towel when squeezing the liquid from the potatoes. Serves 4

  3 pounds Yukon Gold potatoes, peeled
      Coarse salt and freshly ground pepper
  2 tablespoons olive oil

Preheat oven to 400°F. Shred potatoes on the large holes of a box grater. Wrap in cheesecloth; squeeze out as much liquid as possible. Place potatoes in a bowl; toss with 1½ teaspoons salt and 1 teaspoon pepper.

Heat 1 tablespoon oil in a 10-inch ovenproof sauté pan over medium-low. Spread potatoes evenly in pan; press with a spatula to flatten. Cook until underside is golden and turning crisp, about 18 minutes. Remove from heat.

Invert potato cake onto a large plate or a platter; slide back into pan. Return to heat, and spoon remaining tablespoon oil around edges of pan. Cook until other side begins to turn crisp, about 10 minutes, shaking pan several times to loosen cake.

Transfer to oven and bake until potatoes are cooked through (insert a sharp knife into the center to make sure potatoes are tender), about 10 minutes. Invert onto a cutting board or platter. Serve hot; cut into wedges.

Braised Red Cabbage

Blue-black juniper berries have an herbal quality that pairs particularly well with duck in this menu. Before being used in cooking, they are usually crushed to release their flavor and aroma. Serves 4

   1 tablespoon olive oil
   1 red onion, thinly sliced
 15 juniper berries, crushed with the side of a large knife
   1 head red cabbage, halved lengthwise, core removed, thinly sliced
   3 tablespoons red wine vinegar
 1½ cups chicken stock, homemade (see page 260) or low-sodium store-bought
     Coarse salt

Heat oil in a 10-inch high-sided sauté pan over medium. Cook onion until tender, stirring occasionally, 3 to 4 minutes. Stir in juniper berries, then add cabbage and vinegar. Add stock and a large pinch of salt, and bring to a simmer. Reduce heat to medium-low, and simmer until cabbage is just tender, stirring occasionally, 25 to 30 minutes. Season with salt before serving.

Hazelnut Brittle over Ice Cream

Coarse sea salt, such as Fleur de Sel or Maldon, is an essential component of this easy brittle—it flavors the caramel base and adds more crunch on top. Serves 4

  ½ cup sugar
  2 tablespoons water
  1 cup (4 ounces) blanched hazelnuts, toasted (see page 260)
  ¼ teaspoon coarse sea salt, plus more for sprinkling
  ½ teaspoon pure vanilla extract
  1 pint best-quality vanilla ice cream
  1 bar (3.5 ounces) dark chocolate, preferably 61% cacao, broken into pieces

Place a large piece of parchment paper on a work surface. Cook sugar and the water, stirring, in a small saucepan over medium, until sugar dissolves. Stop stirring; continue cooking, washing down sides of pan with a wet pastry brush to prevent crystals from forming and swirling pan until syrup is amber, 6 to 8 minutes. Remove from heat.

Stir in nuts, salt, and vanilla. Pour mixture onto parchment. Using a heatproof flexible spatula, gently press into an even layer. Sprinkle with sea salt. Let cool 20 minutes; break into pieces. To serve, scoop ice cream into four bowls, and top with brittle and chocolate.

{ Scoops of vanilla ice cream are topped with an easy homemade brittle and pieces of dark chocolate for a quick-assembly dessert.

Versatile and ready for cooking, sausage is a reliable choice for dinner on the quick; sliced red onion sautéed alongside is used to make a flavorful pan gravy. The hearty side dishes are also easy to prepare: When finely shredded, tender Tuscan kale needs no cooking, just a few seasonings to make a tasty winter salad. Yorkshire puddings are whisked together in a bowl, then baked in ramekins.

MENU 11

Sausages with Red-Onion Gravy
Rosemary Yorkshire Puddings
Shredded Tuscan Kale Salad
Spiced Prunes in Red Wine

PREPARATION SCHEDULE

1. Make pudding batter, and let rest.
2. Cook prunes; shred kale, and mix dressing.
3. Bake puddings.
4. Meanwhile, cook sausages and make gravy.
5. Add kale and cheese to dressing.

Sausages with Red-Onion Gravy

Serves 4

- 1 tablespoon extra-virgin olive oil
- 8 sweet Italian sausages (2 pounds total)
- 1 pound red onions, cut into ½-inch-thick slices (2½ cups)
- 1 tablespoon all-purpose flour
- 1¼ cups chicken stock, homemade (see page 260) or low-sodium store-bought
- 2 tablespoons red wine vinegar
  Coarse salt and freshly ground pepper

Heat oil in a large skillet over medium-high until hot but not smoking. Add sausages in a single layer. Brown them on one side, about 4 minutes, then add onions, nestling them around sausages. Turn sausages, and cook on opposite side until browned, about 4 minutes.

Reduce heat to medium-low; cook, stirring onions occasionally and turning sausages as necessary, until onions are tender and sausages are cooked through, 8 to 10 minutes. Transfer sausages to a plate (leave onions in skillet); tent with parchment, then foil, to keep warm.

Raise heat to medium-high. Add flour to pan; cook, stirring, 1 minute. Whisk in stock and bring to a simmer, then stir in vinegar. Season with salt and pepper. (You should have 2 cups gravy.) Divide sausages among plates; spoon gravy over.

Rosemary Yorkshire Puddings

Traditionally served as an accompaniment to prime rib, these savory British puddings—similar to popovers—are also delicious with other meats, including sausage. Serves 4

- ¾ cup all-purpose flour
  Coarse salt
- 1½ teaspoons finely chopped fresh rosemary
- 2 large eggs, lightly beaten
- ⅔ cup milk
- 1 tablespoon olive oil or safflower oil, for dishes

Preheat oven to 400°F. Whisk together flour, ½ teaspoon salt, and the rosemary in a medium bowl; make a well in the center, and add eggs and half the milk. Use a fork to gradually combine ingredients, working from the inside out; continue until all flour is incorporated and batter is smooth and stiff. Stir in remaining milk; cover with plastic wrap, and let rest 20 minutes.

Divide oil among four 8-ounce ramekins or custard cups, swirling to coat inside of each surface, and place on a rimmed baking sheet. Heat in the oven until very hot, about 5 minutes.

Divide batter among ramekins, filling each about one-third full. Bake, rotating sheet halfway through, until batter is puffed and golden brown, 25 to 30 minutes. Remove from oven. To unmold, carefully run a butter or table knife around edges and bottom to loosen, then invert each pudding onto a plate. Serve immediately.

Shredded Tuscan Kale Salad

Other names for Tuscan kale include cavolo nero, lacinata kale, and dino kale. If you are unable to find it, substitute savoy cabbage, spinach, or tatsoi, which are similar in texture and flavor (regular kale can be too tough and bitter for serving this way). Serves 4

1 bunch Tuscan kale, finely shredded
1 garlic clove, minced
 Coarse salt and freshly ground pepper
2 tablespoons fresh lemon juice
2 tablespoons extra-virgin olive oil
¼ cup plus 2 tablespoons finely grated Parmigiano-Reggiano cheese (1 ounce)

To shred kale, use a sharp knife to slice leaves very thinly crosswise, stacking them in batches as you work. Whisk together garlic, ¾ teaspoon salt, the lemon juice, and oil in a large bowl; let stand at least 5 minutes (or up to 1 hour). Add the kale, and toss to combine thoroughly; season with pepper.

Add all but 1 tablespoon cheese to kale mixture, and toss to combine. Sprinkle remaining cheese over the top, and serve.

Spiced Prunes in Red Wine

If you don't have cheesecloth, you can simply add the whole spices to the pot; remove the cinnamon stick with the lemon peel and leave the cloves and peppercorns behind when spooning out prunes and poaching liquid. Serves 4

3 whole cloves
6 whole black peppercorns
1 cinnamon stick
2 strips (½ inch by 2 inches) lemon zest (leaving bitter white pith behind)
2 cups dry red wine, such as pinot noir or merlot
½ cup sugar
20 pitted prunes
¼ cup mascarpone cheese (2 ounces), for serving
 Wheatmeal cookies, for serving (optional)

Wrap cloves, peppercorns, and cinnamon in a small piece of cheesecloth; tie with kitchen twine. Add to a 4-quart saucepan along with lemon peel, wine, sugar, and prunes. Bring to a boil over medium-high heat; reduce to a simmer. Cook until prunes have softened and the liquid is reduced but not syrupy, 16 to 18 minutes. Remove from heat.

Using tongs, lift out and discard cheesecloth bundle and lemon peel. Divide prunes and liquid among four shallow bowls, and dollop mascarpone on top of each portion. Serve cookies alongside, if desired.

Prunes become soft and ultra-tender after simmering in red wine redolent of warm spices and lemon. Other dried fruit—figs, dates, even pears—would also be delicious prepared this way. Serve with wheatmeal cookies (shortbread and biscotti are also good options) as well as wine left over from cooking.

{ A cold-weather soup doesn't have to be simmered on the stove for hours to be delicious and nourishing. Fortified with fresh vegetables and a few aromatics, beef stock (from your freezer or the grocer) is cooked briefly to concentrate its flavor; wonton wrappers make easy work of homemade dumplings.

Chicken Liver Mousse with Toast Points
Beef Broth with Leeks, Lemon, and Thyme
Mushroom Dumplings
Blood Oranges and Pomegranates

PREPARATION SCHEDULE

1. Make mousse, and chill; toast bread, and cut into triangles.

2. Cook dumpling filling, and let cool; make pomegranate juice.

3. Serve mousse; bring a pot of water to a boil.

4. Simmer broth; fill dumplings.

5. Assemble dessert just before serving.

Beef Broth with Leeks, Lemon, and Thyme

The key to this simple soup is the quality of the beef stock; homemade is best, but a good-quality supermarket brand makes a fine substitute. Dumplings add just enough heft to turn the soup into a main course, while lemon zest is an unexpected and bright addition. Use a vegetable peeler to remove four strips of lemon peel, leaving the bitter white pith behind, then slice with a sharp knife as thinly as possible. Serves 4

- 4 cups beef stock, homemade (see page 261) or low-sodium store-bought
- 4 cups water
- 1 leek, white and pale-green parts only, cut into 1-inch pieces (1 cup), washed well and drained (see page 260)
- 2 carrots, peeled and cut into 2-inch pieces (¾ cup)
- 3 celery stalks, thinly sliced (¾ cup)
- 2 garlic cloves, halved lengthwise
- 3 strips lemon zest (3 to 4 inches long), cut into very fine julienne (2 tablespoons)
- 1 tablespoon fresh thyme leaves
  Coarse salt and freshly ground pepper
  Mushroom Dumplings

Combine the stock and water in a 4-quart saucepan, and stir in the leek, carrots, celery, garlic, lemon zest, and thyme. Bring to a boil over high heat, then reduce to medium; cook, partially covered, at a gentle simmer until carrots are just tender when pierced with the tip of a sharp knife, 7 to 9 minutes. Season with salt and pepper (remove lemon peel and garlic cloves). Ladle into shallow bowls, and add dumplings, dividing evenly.

Mushroom Dumplings

The dumplings are also delicious on their own, without the broth, as an appetizer or main course (double the recipe); toss with melted butter before serving. Serves 4

- 2 tablespoons unsalted butter
- 6 ounces cremini mushrooms, trimmed and finely chopped (about 1¾ cups)
- ½ yellow onion, finely chopped (about ½ cup)
  Coarse salt and freshly ground pepper
- 2 tablespoons cream cheese, softened
- 2 tablespoons finely chopped fresh chives
- 1 tablespoon finely chopped fresh flat-leaf parsley
- 16 wonton wrappers (round or square), thawed if frozen

Melt butter in a medium skillet over medium-high heat. Add mushrooms, onion, and a pinch of salt; cook, stirring occasionally, until vegetables are golden and tender, about 7 minutes. Let cool slightly, 5 to 10 minutes. Add cream cheese and stir until combined; stir in chives and parsley, and season with salt and pepper. (You should have about ¾ cup filling.)

To assemble, place about 1 teaspoon filling on one half of each wonton wrapper, and moisten edges of wrapper lightly with water. Fold opposite side of wrapper over to enclose filling, pressing out any air and sealing the edges tightly. Bring the two outside corners together, and press tightly to seal, moistening with more water if necessary.

Bring a large pot of water to a boil, and add salt. Cook wontons until wrapper is tender and filling is heated through, about 3 minutes. Remove with a slotted spoon. Serve immediately.

A help-yourself appetizer allows guests to mingle while you finish cooking the rest of the meal. Here, savory chicken liver mousse, currant jelly, and toast points are set on a round platter board for easy assembly.

Chicken Liver Mousse with Toast Points

The flavorful mousse is served with toast points, but good-quality crackers are an easy alternative. Dry sherry, marsala, or port can be used in place of Madeira. Serves 4

- 2 tablespoons safflower or other neutral-tasting oil
- ½ pound chicken livers, stringy membranes removed with a small knife (or ask a butcher to do this for you, if possible)
  Coarse salt and freshly ground pepper
- 1 shallot, minced (about 3 tablespoons)
- 3 sprigs thyme
- 4 tablespoons (½ stick) unsalted butter, room temperature
- 1 teaspoon Madeira
- 4 to 6 slices firm white sandwich bread, lightly toasted
  Red currant jelly, for serving

Heat oil in a large skillet over medium-high. Rinse livers, and pat dry with a paper towel; add to pan, and season both sides with salt and pepper. Cook until browned on each side but still pink in the center, 1½ to 2 minutes per side (do not overcook). Transfer to a plate with a slotted spoon, and let cool.

Reduce heat to medium. Add shallot and thyme to pan; cook, stirring occasionally, until shallot is softened and golden, about 3 minutes. Transfer shallot to plate with livers; discard thyme.

Puree livers, shallot, butter, Madeira, and 1 teaspoon salt in a food processor until smooth, stopping and scraping down the sides with a flexible spatula as needed. Transfer the mixture to a serving dish, and cover with plastic wrap. Refrigerate 30 minutes.

Meanwhile, trim off crusts from toasted bread, and cut each slice into 4 triangles. Serve mousse with toast points and jelly.

Mousses and Pâtés

Despite their French pedigree, mousses and pâtés are not terribly complicated to prepare. They can also be very affordable, especially when made with inexpensive cuts of meat, such as chicken livers. There are myriad options to choose from, some fancier than others. Besides chicken liver, other common main ingredients are duck, smoked salmon, or trout, and there are many vegetarian versions that you can make or buy. You'll want to serve these spreads with some flavorful accompaniments; pairings that combine savory with sweet are one way to go. Currant jelly complements the seasonings in the mousse here, but fig or quince preserves would work as well. Or you could offer a few tart components, such as cornichons or other pickled vegetables, along with zesty mustards or chutneys, which will offset the richness of the mousse or pâté. Finally, you'll need something on which to spread. Toast points are traditional, but slices of baguette or other rustic bread, or even assorted crackers or flatbreads, are worthy alternatives.

Seeding and Juicing Pomegranates

Pomegranates are in season from October through January. The best fruits have brightly colored and unblemished skin, and are heavy for their size (which means the jewel-like seeds inside are at their juiciest). It's quick and easy work to extract the seeds: Halve or quarter the fruit, then rest the pieces in a bowl, cut sides down. Using the back of a wooden spoon, whack the fruit a few times to release the seeds (if necessary, you can scrape out any seeds that remain attached). The fruit's ruby-red juice can easily stain clothing and work surfaces; protect against splatters by wearing clean kitchen gloves and an apron, and cover your counter with waxed paper or plastic wrap. Use a citrus juicer or reamer to extract juice from the seeds.

Blood Oranges and Pomegranates

There are great options for fresh fruit desserts in winter, including this gorgeous example. Serves 4

- 3 blood oranges
- 1 tablespoon Grand Marnier or other orange-flavored liqueur
- 2 teaspoons fresh pomegranate juice
- ½ cup pomegranate seeds

Use a vegetable peeler to remove 2 strips of zest from an orange, leaving the bitter white pith behind; cut into very fine julienne with a sharp knife. Combine zest in a small bowl with Grand Marnier and pomegranate juice, and let stand about 10 minutes.

Meanwhile, peel all oranges with a paring knife; holding each orange over a bowl, cut between membranes to remove whole segments, letting them drop into the bowl.

To serve, divide orange segments and pomegranate seeds evenly among four shallow bowls; spoon some zest mixture over each portion.

A crimson dessert would likely be eye-catching (and mouthwatering) in any setting, but it is especially appropriate for a holiday meal when served in gold-rimmed clear glass bowls resting on hem-stitched white napkins and a deep red tablecloth.

Preparing a celebratory dinner need not be taxing, as demonstrated by this indulgent two-course meal. You'll want to preserve the flavor and tender texture of the filet, however, since it's admittedly an expensive cut. Potatoes, a natural companion for beef, are boiled, then pureed with bay leaf–scented tiny onions simmered in a port-rich sauce that thickens to a delicious glaze.

Spice-Rubbed Beef Filets
Port-Glazed Pearl Onions
Golden Potato Puree
Chocolate Truffles

PREPARATION SCHEDULE

1. Make truffles, and refrigerate.
2. Simmer and glaze onions.
3. Meanwhile, boil potatoes, and steep bay leaf in milk.
4. Rub filets with spice crust, and sear.
5. Puree potatoes while beef is resting.

Spice-Rubbed Beef Filets

For this recipe, the spices need to be ground very fine to blend thoroughly with the salt; an electric spice grinder works best. Serves 4

2 whole star anise
1 teaspoon whole black peppercorns
1½ teaspoons coarse salt
4 filets mignon (each 6 ounces and 2 inches thick)
3 tablespoons olive oil
Golden Potato Puree

Preheat oven to 450°F. Finely grind star anise, peppercorns, and salt in a spice grinder (or a clean coffee grinder). Pat dry beef with paper towels, then rub spice mixture all over beef to coat evenly.

Heat oil in a large ovenproof sauté pan over medium-high until hot but not smoking. Sear filets until a deep brown crust forms on the first sides, about 2 minutes; flip beef, and cook until a crust forms on the other sides, about 2 minutes more. Transfer to oven and cook until an instant-read thermometer inserted in thickest part registers 125°F for medium-rare, about 10 minutes.

To serve, divide potato puree evenly among four plates, and place a filet on top of each. Spoon onions and their glaze over beef and potatoes.

Golden Potato Puree

A ricer will produce the smoothest, fluffiest potatoes, but you can use a handheld masher instead. Serves 4

1½ pounds Yukon Gold potatoes
Coarse salt and freshly ground pepper
⅓ cup milk
1 dried bay leaf
1 tablespoon unsalted butter

Peel the potatoes, then cut into quarters (or eighths if large). Place in a 4-quart saucepan, and cover with cold water by 2 inches. Bring to a boil over high heat; add ½ teaspoon salt. Reduce heat to medium, and simmer until potatoes are tender when pierced with a fork, about 15 minutes.

Meanwhile, bring milk and bay leaf just to a simmer in a small saucepan over medium-high heat, and turn off heat. Keep covered until ready to use.

Drain potatoes, reserving ¼ cup cooking water. Return potatoes to hot pan for a few minutes to dry out, then pass the potatoes through a ricer (or mash by hand). Remove bay leaf from milk, and discard. Stir milk and butter into the potatoes until combined. Add enough of the reserved cooking water, 1 tablespoon at a time, and stir until potatoes have reached desired consistency. Season with salt and pepper. Serve warm.

Port-Glazed Pearl Onions

Red pearl onions provide rosy color, but white ones work just as well. To peel the onions, blanch them in a pot of boiling water for one minute, then drain and run under cold water until cool enough to handle. Snip off the root ends with a paring knife, and squeeze—the onions should pop out easily. Serves 4

  2   cups pearl onions (about 10 ounces), peeled
  1½ cups tawny port
  1   tablespoon sugar
  1   cup beef stock, homemade (see page 261) or low-sodium store-bought
  1   tablespoon red wine vinegar
  2   tablespoons unsalted butter
      Coarse salt and freshly ground pepper

Bring onions and port to a simmer in a medium sauté pan over medium heat; cook, stirring occasionally, until liquid is reduced to a thin syrup, about 10 minutes.

Add sugar, and cook until dissolved, about 1 minute. Pour in stock and vinegar, and simmer (do not boil) until reduced and thickened, and the onions are tender, about 10 minutes more. Add butter, stirring until melted; season with salt and pepper. Serve hot.

Chocolate Truffles

You can roll the truffles in one, two, or all three of the coatings below (adapting amounts accordingly). Makes 1 dozen

  2   ounces roasted, salted pistachios, chopped
  3   tablespoons best-quality unsweetened Dutch-process cocoa powder
  2   ounces peanut brittle, finely chopped
  5   ounces bittersweet chocolate, preferably 61% cacao, finely chopped
  ¼   cup milk
  1   tablespoon unsalted butter
  1   tablespoon brandy

Prepare an ice-water bath. Line a baking sheet with parchment. Place pistachios, cocoa powder, and brittle in separate bowls. Place chocolate in a heatproof bowl. Bring milk and butter just to a simmer in a saucepan; pour over chocolate, and whisk until smooth. Whisk in brandy.

Set bowl in ice bath; whisk constantly, scraping sides of bowl, until mixture is thick enough to scoop with a spoon, about 5 minutes. Use a mini ice-cream scoop (or a teaspoon) to form mixture into balls, dropping them into a coating as you go; roll to cover.

Transfer to prepared baking sheet and refrigerate until set, at least 10 minutes. (Truffles will keep up to 1 week in the refrigerator; store in a single layer in an airtight container.)

Chocolate truffles are much easier to make from scratch than you might imagine. Chilling the chocolate mixture in an ice-water bath expedites the process; once rolled and coated, the truffles are left to set in the refrigerator. Serve in confectionery papers for festive occasions, with glasses of port.

basics

CROSTINI
Place baguette slices on a baking sheet and brush both sides lightly with olive oil. Bake in a 400°F oven until golden brown, about 10 minutes, flipping once halfway through. Transfer to a wire rack to cool.

BREAD CRUMBS
Trim off crusts from a loaf of bread (Pullman, baguette, or other type), and tear the bread into large pieces. Pulse in a food processor to form coarse or fine crumbs, as desired. (For dried bread crumbs, toast the crumbs in a 250°F oven 12 to 15 minutes.) Leftover bread crumbs can be frozen, in an airtight container, for months.

TOASTING NUTS
Spread nuts on a rimmed baking sheet and toast in a 350°F oven until fragrant and darkened slightly, 7 to 10 minutes, tossing occasionally. Transfer to a plate to cool.

PEELING HAZELNUTS
Spread raw (shelled) hazelnuts in a single layer on a rimmed baking sheet; bake in a 275°F oven until skins crack, 25 to 30 minutes. Remove from oven and wrap in a clean kitchen towel; let steam 5 minutes, then rub off the papery skins with the towel (don't worry if a few skins remain).

TOASTING SESAME SEEDS
Heat seeds in a small skillet over medium, shaking the pan occasionally, until golden, 2 to 3 minutes (be careful not to let them burn). Transfer to a plate to cool.

CLEANING MUSSELS
Use a knife or your fingers to pull away the beards (tough fibers) from the mussels, and discard. Holding them under cold running water, scrub mussels with a stiff-bristle brush, then soak in cold water until ready to use, up to 30 minutes. When ready to use, lift shells out of water, leaving sediment behind (do not drain in a colander).

CLEANING CLAMS
Holding under cold running water, scrub clams with a stiff-bristle brush, then place in a bowl of cold water and add a handful of cornmeal (which helps draw out the grit) for 15 to 30 minutes; lift clams from water, and rinse. When ready to use, lift shells out of water, leaving sediment behind (do not drain in a colander).

PEELING AND DEVEINING SHRIMP
Holding shrimp by the tail, peel shell from inside curve with your fingers, leaving tail intact (or remove, if desired). Gently run a paring knife from head to tail along the center of the back to expose the vein. Then use the knife to remove the blackish "vein" in one piece.

WASHING LEEKS
Trim and discard root ends and dark green parts from leeks. Cut leeks into pieces of desired size, then place in a bowl; wash leeks in several changes of cold water, swishing to loosen grit, until you no longer see any grit in bottom of bowl. Lift leeks out of water, and dry on a clean kitchen towel (or paper towels).

CHICKEN STOCK
Makes about 2½ quarts

- 5 pounds assorted chicken parts (backs, necks, and wings)
- 2 medium carrots, cut into 1-inch pieces
- 2 large celery stalks, cut into 1-inch pieces
- 2 medium onions, cut into eighths
- 1 dried bay leaf
- 1 teaspoon whole black peppercorns

Place chicken parts in an 8-quart stockpot and add enough water to cover by 1 inch (about 3 quarts). Bring to a boil over medium-high heat, using a ladle or large spoon to skim foam from surface. Add carrots, celery, onions, bay leaf, and peppercorns, and reduce heat to a bare simmer. Cook, skimming frequently, about 2 hours.

Strain stock through a fine sieve (preferably lined with cheesecloth) into a large heatproof bowl or another pot, pressing on solids with a wooden spoon to release as much liquid as possible (discard solids). Skim off fat if using immediately, or let cool completely (an ice-water bath speeds this process) before transferring to airtight containers. Refrigerate at least 6 hours to allow fat to accumulate at the top. With a large spoon, remove and discard fat before using or storing stock. Stock can be refrigerated in airtight containers for up to three days or frozen for up to six months; thaw in the refrigerator before using.

BEEF STOCK
Makes about 3 quarts

- 6   pounds beef bone-in short ribs, trimmed of excess fat
    Coarse salt and freshly ground pepper
- 1   can (28 ounces) whole peeled tomatoes, coarsely chopped, juice reserved
- 2   dried bay leaves
- 1   small bunch fresh thyme
- 10 whole black peppercorns

Preheat oven to 450°F. Arrange ribs in a large roasting pan; sprinkle generously with salt and pepper. Roast until well browned, turning ribs halfway through, about 1½ hours.

Transfer ribs to an 8-quart stockpot and add enough water to cover by 1 inch (about 3 quarts). Pour off and discard fat from roasting pan. Pour 1 cup water into pan. Bring to a boil over medium-high heat, scraping any browned bits from the bottom with a wooden spoon, until water is reduced by half. Transfer liquid and bits to stockpot. Add tomatoes and their juice, bay leaves, thyme, and peppercorns.

Bring mixture to a simmer over high heat (do not boil). Reduce heat until liquid is at a gentle simmer, and place a smaller pot lid directly on surface of stock to keep ingredients submerged; cook until meat is very tender and pulls away from the bone, about 1½ hours. Skim foam from surface with a ladle or large spoon as needed. Remove ribs from pot. (Let cool slightly, then pull meat from the bones and save for another use; refrigerate, covered, up to 3 days.)

Strain stock through a fine sieve (preferably lined with cheesecloth) into a large heatproof bowl or another pot, pressing on solids with a wooden spoon to release as much liquid as possible (discard solids). Skim off fat if using immediately, or let cool completely (an ice-water bath speeds the process) before transferring to airtight containers. Refrigerate at least 6 hours to allow fat to accumulate at the top. With a large spoon, remove and discard fat before using or storing stock.

Save the meat pulled from the bones to make fillings for tacos, enchiladas, or quesadillas. Stock can be refrigerated in airtight containers for up to three days or frozen for up to six months; thaw in the refrigerator before using.

VEGETABLE STOCK
Makes about 2 quarts

- 3   tablespoons olive oil
- 1   large onion, coarsely chopped
- 2   large celery stalks, coarsely chopped
- 2   medium carrots, coarsely chopped
- 2   garlic cloves, thinly sliced
- 10 cups water
- 8   sprigs flat-leaf parsley
- 8   sprigs basil
- 4   sprigs thyme
- 1   dried bay leaf
- ¼   teaspoon whole black peppercorns
    Coarse salt and freshly ground pepper

Heat oil in a 6-quart stockpot over medium. Add onion; cook, stirring often, until golden brown, 10 to 15 minutes. Add celery, carrots, and garlic. Cook, stirring occasionally, until vegetables are tender, about 10 minutes.

Stir in the water, herbs, and peppercorns; season with salt and pepper. Bring to a boil. Reduce heat, and simmer 1 hour.

Strain stock through a fine sieve (preferably lined with cheesecloth) into a large heatproof bowl or another pot, pressing on solids with a wooden spoon to extract as much liquid as possible (discard solids). Use immediately, or let cool completely before storing in airtight containers. Stock can be refrigerated in airtight containers up to three days or frozen for up to six months; thaw in the refrigerator before using.

starters

mains

SPRING

Baby Lamb Chops with Lemon Strips, 15

Pasta with Mint Pesto and Fava, 21

Turkey and Pancetta Meatballs, 22

Roast Salmon and Potatoes with Mustard-Herb Butter, 27

Roast Beef with Horseradish Sauce, 31

Herbed Lamb and Pita, 35

Shrimp in Saffron Broth, 39

Strip Steak with Chimichurri, 43

Catfish Po'boys, 47

Coconut Poached Chicken, 51

Pasta Shards with Fresh Herbs, 55

Poached Eggs with Brown Butter, 55

Prosciutto-Wrapped Pork Cutlets, 61

Pan-Roasted Chicken Pieces, 65

Baked Flounder with Lemons and Onions, 69

SUMMER

Pancetta Cheeseburgers, 77

Broiled Black-Pepper Tofu, 81

Salmon with Creamy Leeks, 85

Honey-Glazed Chicken Skewers, 89

Tender Shredded Pork, 95

Spicy Stir-Fried Shrimp, 100

Grilled Steak with Blue Cheese Potatoes, 105

Grilled Striped Bass, 111

Herbed Turkey Burgers, 115

Seared Tuna in Tomato-Basil Sauce, 119

Grilled Pork Paillards, 123

Chicken in Tonnato Sauce, 127

Pork Kebabs with Thyme, 133

FALL

Roasted Pork with Sage and Garlic, 143

Tomato, Eggplant, and Mozzarella Stacks, 147

Trout with Almonds and Orange, 151

Grilled Spiced Lamb Chops, 155

Chicken Paillards with Walnut Sauce, 159

Skillet Rib-Eye Steaks, 163

Cheese Flautas with Cilantro Pesto, 167

Miso-Glazed Fish Fillets, 171

Quail with Figs and Pine Nuts, 175

Steamed Mussels and Clams in Smoky Tomato Broth, 181

Pork Chops with Sautéed Apples and Onion, 187

Braised Chicken Marsala, 191

Bay Scallops with Lemon Butter and Herbs, 195

WINTER

Crisp Ham and Cheese Sandwiches, 205

Hanger Steak with Caramelized Shallots, 207

Broiled Red Snapper, 213

Crisp Pork Cutlets, 217

Spaghetti with Clams, 221

Hoisin-Glazed Hens, 225

Roast Chicken Breasts in Creamy Tarragon Sauce, 233

Curried Vegetable Potpies, 239

Duck Breast with Fig Sauce, 243

Sausages with Red-Onion Gravy, 247

Mushroom Dumplings, 251

Spice-Rubbed Beef Filets, 257

sides

desserts

SPRING

Vanilla-Poached Rhubarb, 18

Coffee Ice Cream Affogato, 24

Lemon Mousse, 28

Baked Cinnamon Apples, 32

Greek Yogurt with Clementines and Pistachios, 36

Apricot-Almond Ice Cream Sandwiches, 40

Torrijas, 44

Bananas with Caramel Sauce, 48

Minty Green Tea Milkshakes, 52

Tiramisù, 58

Amaretti-Ricotta Sandwiches, 62

Raspberries with Honey and Buttermilk, 66

Bread and Butter Pudding with Strawberries, 70

SUMMER

Coconut-Topped Cupcakes, 78

Baked Apricots with Almond Topping, 82

Raspberry-Mint Gelatin Cups, 86

Espresso Cream Crunch, 92

Tequila-Soaked Lemon Sorbet, 96

Sorbet with Wonton Crisps, 102

Blackberry Red Wine Gelatin, 108

Watermelon-Raspberry Salad, 112

Blackberry Shortbread Squares, 116

Peaches in Honey Syrup, 120

Cherry Ice, 124

Cornmeal Cake with Blueberries and Cream, 130

Cantaloupe Granita, 134

FALL

Pears with Candied Walnuts and Gorgonzola, 144

Glazed Plums with Mascarpone, 148

Sugared Grape and Phyllo Tart, 152

Papaya with Coconut-Lime Yogurt, 156

Goat Cheese–Stuffed Dates, 160

Molten Chocolate-Espresso Cakes, 164

Apple-Cranberry Crumble, 168

Caramelized Persimmons, 172

Frozen Grapes with Sauternes Granita, 178

Dark Chocolate Puddings, 184

Maple Custards, 188

Sautéed Pears in Honey Syrup, 192

Jam-Glazed Hazelnut Mini Cakes, 196

WINTER

Pear and Dried Cherry Baked Custard, 205

Caramel Pudding, 210

Rice Pudding with Candied Kumquats, 214

Cherry Compote over Chocolate Ice Cream, 219

Grapefruit in Moscato, 222

Kiwi Fruit in Jasmine Tea Syrup, 226

Coffee with Cognac and Cardamom, 231

Poached Pears with Chocolate Sauce, 236

Spiced Lemon Cookies, 240

Hazelnut Brittle over Ice Cream, 244

Spiced Prunes in Red Wine, 248

Blood Oranges and Pomegranates, 254

Chocolate Truffles, 258

acknowledgments

It took the collaboration of many individuals to create this collection of wonderful menus, notably deputy food editor Anna Kovel, who, aided by associate editors Allison Hedges and Lesley Stockton, developed and oversaw the testing of the majority of recipes.

Thanks to book editors Ellen Morrissey and Evelyn Battaglia for overseeing the publication of this book from start to finish, and to managing editor Sarah Rutledge Gorman for her keen attention to detail. Thanks as well to art directors William van Roden and Matthew Papa for the beautiful design, as well as Ayesha Patel, Michelle Wong, and Sarah Smart for their impeccable prop styling. A special thanks to the many talented photographers whose work graces these pages (see

below) and to Valerie Shaff for such a lovely cover portrait. And many thanks to others who provided ideas, guidance, and support, among them Jennifer Aaronson, Christine Albano, Shira Bocar, Monita Buchwald, Sarah Carey, Denise Clappi, Christine Cyr, Alison Vanek Devine, Lawrence Diamond, James Dunlinson, Stephanie Fletcher, Catherine Gilbert, Katie Goldberg, Heloise Goodman, Sara Parks, Eric A. Pike, Lucinda Scala Quinn, Megan Rice, and Gael Towey.

This book wouldn't be possible without the teamwork of our longtime partners at Clarkson Potter: Rica Allannic, Amy Boorstein, Angelin Borsics, Doris Cooper, Jenny Frost, Derek Gullino, Mark McCauslin, Marysarah Quinn, Lauren Shakely, and Jane Treuhaft.

photograph credits

Antonis Achilleos, 154, 156, 157

Sang An, 140, 141, 142, 144, 145, 164, 165, 231

Stefan Anderson, 84, 86, 87

Quentin Bacon, 110, 111, 113

James Baigrie, 24, 25

Lisa Cohen, 18

Beatriz Da Costa, 172 (right), 173, 206, 208, 209, 210, 211

Dana Gallagher, 30, 32, 33, 98, 100, 101, 102, 103, 117, 132, 134 (left)

Lisa Hubbard, 220, 222, 223

Gentl & Hyers, 72

John Kernick, 179, 184

John Kernick, 179, 184

Yunhee Kim, 5

Jason Loucas, 2, 6, 38, 40, 41, 54, 56, 58, 59, 60, 61, 62, 63, 126, 128, 130, 131, 198, 224, 226, 227, 228, 229, 230, 242, 244, 245

William Meppem, 118, 120, 121, 122, 124, 125

Johnny Miller, 6, 10, 22 (left), 42, 44, 45, 46, 48, 49, 50, 52, 53, 158, 177, 202, 203, 204, 212, 214, 215, 216, 218, 219, 232, 235, 236, 237, 238, 239, 240, 241, 246, 248, 249, 250, 252, 254, 255, 256, 258, 259

Amy Neunsinger, 114, 116, 134 (right), 135

Marcus Nilsson, 136

Victoria Pearson, 68, 70, 71, 94, 96, 97

Kate Sears, 14, 16, 17, 19, 20, 22 (right), 23, 26, 28, 29, 34, 35, 36, 37, 64, 66, 67, 146, 147, 148, 149, 150, 152, 153, 160, 161, 162, 163, 166, 167, 169, 170, 172 (left), 174, 176, 180, 182, 183, 185, 186, 188, 189, 190, 192, 193, 194, 196, 197

Kirsten Strecker, 76, 78, 79, 80, 82, 83, 88, 89, 90, 91, 92, 93, 104, 105, 106, 107, 108, 109, 205